W9-DAQ-567

THE NORMAN ROCKWELL ALBUM

"Homecoming Soldier."

THE NORMAN ROCKWELL ALBUM

1961
DOUBLEDAY & COMPANY, INC.
GARDEN CITY, NEW YORK

TO MARY
WITH LOVE AND GRATITUDE

DESIGNED BY JOSEPH P. ASCHERL

LIBRARY OF CONGRESS CATALOG CARD NUMBER 61–12573

PRINTED IN THE UNITED STATES OF AMERICA

FIRST EDITION

INTRODUCTION

It is a pleasure to salute a Berkshire neighbor, a fine citizen, and a genial observer of American life. Norman Rockwell is all of these. He is also a national institution. He wears his fame gracefully, and one cannot meet him without believing that he has deserved it. Like his work, his nature is unassuming, generous, and kindly. His many imitators do not seem able to match his quality of heart and his skill of hand. Though he has some detractors, it is probable that they enjoy his work more than they like to admit. From personal experience I know how easy it is to paint yourself in that corner, all in the name of art.

Unfortunately, many supporters of modern painting find it necessary to scorn Norman Rockwell while acclaiming, let us say, Jackson Pollock. Why not admit that they are utterly different and be grateful for both of them? I am glad to have been among the first to champion the work of Pollock, but I am also glad to have stopped pretending, some time ago, that I did not enjoy Rockwell's covers for the *Saturday Evening Post*.

In welcoming two such different painters I am not, of course, following the same standard of judgment. This is appropriate to the separate natures of art and illustration—separate, though they often overlap. Thus Pollock was an artist, though he "illustrated" in his own way some of the dynamism and the tensions of modern life. Rockwell is essentially an illustrator, an extraordinarily gifted one, though his images of homely incident are deceptive in their artlessness. More of this later.

Art and illustration both have their uses, and it is perverse to consider one the enemy of the other. Yet many of Rockwell's admirers use him as a spear-

Rembrandt, *Young Girl at a Half Door.*

Gerard Dou, *Girl at Window.*

head to attack modern art (without any attempt to understand it), while various pundits use him as a whipping boy to deplore the condition of public taste. For reasons that go deep into social history since the French Revolution, people today respond more readily to illustration than to art; and, as a result, the illustrator has too often displaced the artist as a public hero. This is manifestly wrong. To redress the balance, however, we need better understanding of art, not less affection for our illustrators.

Rockwell belongs to a line of humorous genre painters which originated at least as long ago as in seventeenth-century Holland, and perhaps in the marginal amusements of medieval manuscripts. Such painters flourished in the nineteenth century: Spitzweg has never ceased to be a popular idol in Munich, while William Sidney Mount has recently regained the affection of an American public. Yet it is clear today that their respective countrymen, Hans von Marées and Thomas Eakins, dwarf them in imagination and profundity. In much the same way a Teniers plays a minor obbligato to a Rubens, a Brouwer to a Hals, a Gerard Dou to a Rembrandt. Like Spitzweg, Mount, and Rockwell, these lesser painters combine solid craftsmanship with a gently, sometimes wryly, humorous view of life. Their appeal is due partly to what Aristotle called the pleasures of recognition, partly to their own skill of execution, and partly to their possession of a gift which we normally associate today with our best photographers: the sense of the decisive moment.

Humorous genre painting has little to do with "primitive" art, whether the latter is taken at the dreamlike and disquieting level of a *douanier* Rousseau, or at the pleasantly harmless one of a Grandma Moses. "Primitive" art tells its story by exploiting the so-called abstract (but extremely tangible) language of artistic form—that is to say, such elements as color, shape, texture, and rhythm. Genre painting depends much less on these elements, particularly Spitzweg's and Rockwell's. The chief aim of such painting is to portray an everyday incident chosen for its interest as such, and to let it speak for itself. When, for example, Gerard Dou paints a girl at a window, we are fascinated

"Saying Grace."

Édouard Manet, *The Guitar Player.*

by her expression (what is going to happen?), by her clothes, by what is on the window sill. Painting the same subject, Rembrandt envelops us in the magic of human personality. Dou's girl is, as we say, "typical"; Rembrandt's, being absolutely untypical, is unique. Rembrandt's art expands; Dou's seems to contract. All the same, we treasure the smaller blessings that Dou gives us.

Since genre painters through the ages have had the same basic, and limited, intention, it should not surprise us that they resemble one another, despite disparities of environment. Great artists, on the other hand, differ as widely as their times (except to the extent that greatness itself, being timeless, is a link across time). We should no more expect Rockwell to resemble Pollock than Dou, Rembrandt; or Spitzweg, Hans von Marées. If we add a regional difference, we should no more expect Rockwell to resemble Picasso than Dou, Rubens; or Spitzweg, Manet.

I have referred above to the apparent artlessness of Rockwell's homely images. They are the result of rigorous selection, meticulous craftsmanship, and hard work. His drawings, too little known, show his method. They suggest that illustration even in its purest form needs, and profits from, an artistic base.

S. Lane Faison, Jr.
Chairman, Art Department, Williams College
Director, Lawrence Art Museum, Williams College

Karl Spitzweg, *The Feathered Intruder.*

CONTENTS

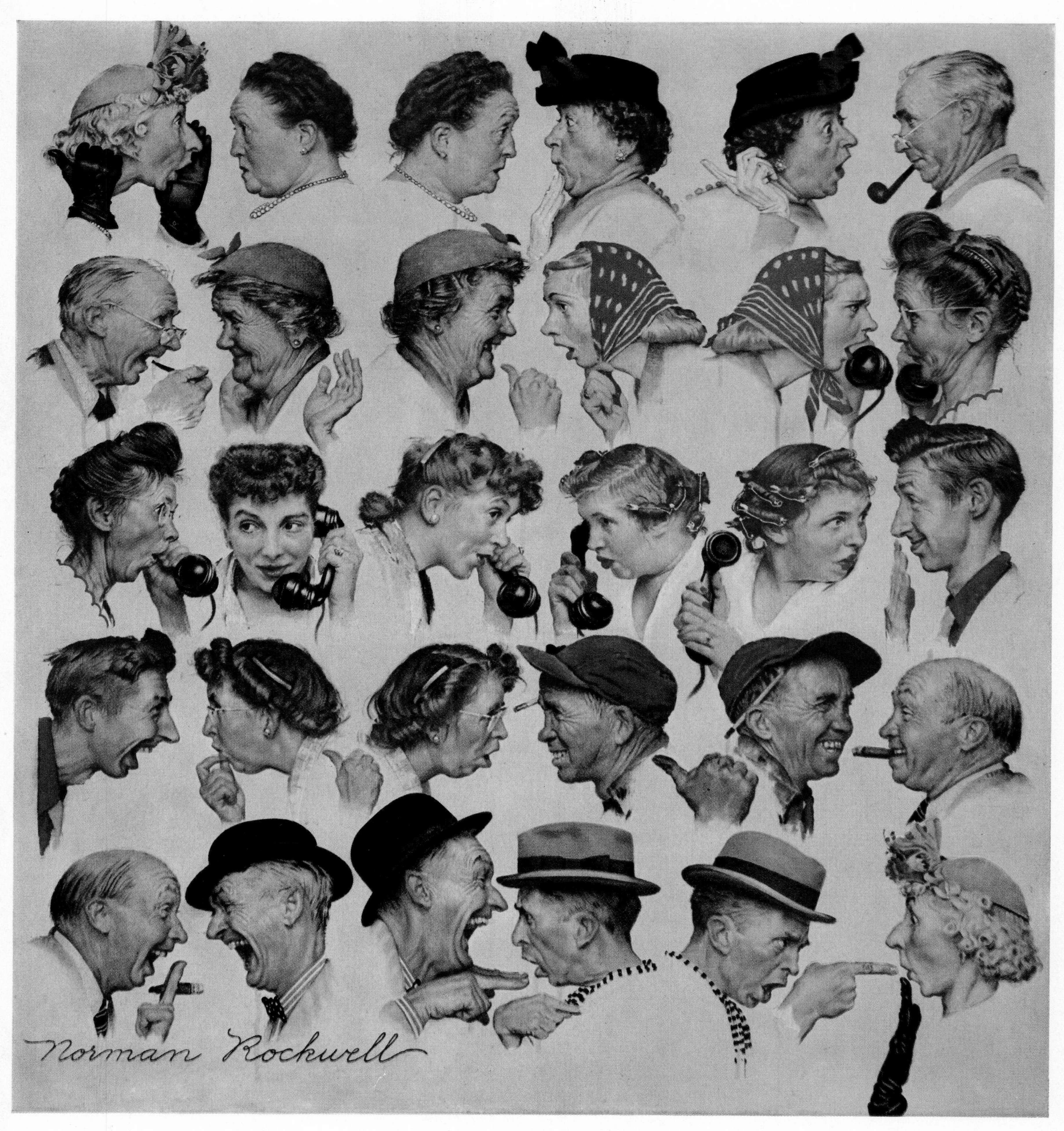

"The Gossips."

PREFACE

The scope of Norman Rockwell's unique talent is suggested by an incident that began one Saturday morning in 1951, when I took my sons to a Children's Concert given by the Philadelphia Orchestra. We lunched at the Juniper Street automat, the children's favorite restaurant. Single food portions, in separate compartments, were displayed behind small glass doors. These opened when the required number of nickels were dropped in a slot and a little knob was turned. After the children had shopped with their fistfuls of coins, we maneuvered our trays onto a table and sat down. Near us was an Amish family, their heads bowed in silent grace. I'm afraid we gawked, but it didn't occur to me that what we saw could be the subject of a magazine cover.

Months later Norman Rockwell came to Philadelphia with some sketches. One was of his memorable painting on page 7 portraying an old lady and a little boy saying grace in an unpretentious restaurant. Millions of our readers voted this quietly compelling canvas their favorite. I asked Norman where he got the idea. He said that some lady from West Philadelphia had written him about seeing an Amish family at grace in an automat restaurant, and he thought he would try a sketch.

Just as great writers put into words the unexpressed thoughts of mankind, so great painters exalt the commonplace, showing to us the world we have stared at with blind eyes. I never knew Paris streets—though I lived on one for two years—until I saw Utrillo's paintings. The landscapes of Cézanne and van Gogh led me to the loveliness of the French countryside.

Norman, too, has this superb gift, the ability to reveal the deeper meaning of what you see. A few sentences in a letter, filtered through his sensitive feeling for humanity, prompted all the marvelous complexities of this great narrative painting. The original now hangs on my office wall, causing many of my visitors to pause a moment in silent wonder. No one has to explain it to them; no guide is needed for Norman's work. The warmth of his understanding reaches them. People *experience* his paintings.

Well, here's a handsome book of the wonderful work that has brought pleasure to generations of Americans. Norman's humor, his joy in living, and his deep concern for people are on every page. For me, part of the delight and charm of these scenes is Norman himself. When showing his sketches, his enthusiasm often takes over, and he begins to act out the main characters. I've seen few comparable mimics. He can be the doubting adolescent, the forbidding umpire, or the charwoman—all with convincing reality. Perhaps this skill explains his mastery of human gesture. More than six hundred years ago Dante said, "Who paints a figure, if he cannot be it, cannot draw it."

I suppose we all have our favorite Rockwells. Ben Hibbs has always liked the "Homecoming Soldier" on page 2. My choice is the remarkable "Gossips" on page 10, which was painted in 1948. I like it better than any other magazine cover. It began to take form, not as shown here, but as two old ladies talking over a fence. Then, for a time, there were ten heads, in the shape of a question mark. At different times Norman considered, forgot, worried, and perfected the painting, so that thirteen years passed before he finally let us have the version that satisfied him. Like all dedicated artists, Norman expects each new painting to be better than the last. He's a fingernail-biter when a finished canvas is on its way—until I phone him that it has arrived, it's okay, and it's wonderful. Norman says "Fine," and then, "Boy, wait'll you see the one I'm working on now."

KENNETH STUART
Art Editor, The Saturday Evening POST

"Ken Stuart," by NR.

THE NORMAN ROCKWELL ALBUM

CHRONOLOGY

Curls and lace: baby Norman, age two.

1894 February 3. The back bedroom of a shabby brownstone in New York City. I arrive in the world feet first at 2:00 A.M.

1899 After attending Admiral Dewey's Triumphal Parade in a gocart, I make childish drawings of America's warships.

1903 We move from New York City to suburban Mamaroneck. To me it is a move from the grim, smoky city to the wide, green country.

1904 I discover my monstrous Adam's apple, narrow shoulders, long neck, and pigeon toes. My parents have me fitted for correctional shoes. But when my father reads Dickens to the family by gaslight, I forget my shortcomings and express my sympathy for Little Nell and Oliver Twist and my fear of the villains Fagin and Bill Sykes by drawing pictures of them.

1906 I am fitted with round spectacles and acquire the nickname Moonface, or Mooney. I fill the margins of my schoolbooks with sketches.

High-button shoes and a middy blouse: myself and my brother Jarvis, 1900.

1899. A Victorian family: my mother and father, myself and Jarvis.

1907 My older brother Jarvis is a strapping athlete. To compensate for my lack of athletic prowess, I begin to take my drawing seriously. I decide to become an illustrator.

1909 Wednesdays and Saturdays I commute by trolley to New York City to attend the Chase School of Fine and Applied Art.

1910 I quit high school in my sophomore year and study full time at the National Academy of Design and at the Art Students League under George Bridgman and Thomas Fogarty.

1911 I sign my name in blood, swearing never to prostitute my art, never to do advertising jobs, never to allow myself to earn more than $50 a week. I win a scholarship to Thomas Fogarty's illustration class at the League but never use it. Instead I start illustrating. I am known as the "Boy Illustrator."

George Bridgman. Sketched by McCoy, a fellow student.

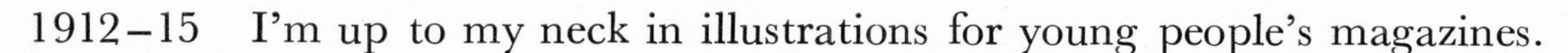

1912–15 I'm up to my neck in illustrations for young people's magazines.

1916 I attempt a cover for the *Saturday Evening Post.* The editor accepts it and okays two idea sketches. Jubilation! I marry Irene O'Connor. I begin to do more work for adult magazines, less for young people's magazines.

1917 Overcome with patriotism, I enlist in the Navy. My duties in Special Services are light, so I continue painting covers and illustrations. I am making more money than an admiral.

1918 I paint a portrait of my commanding officer and receive an early, special discharge.

1919 I paint my first advertisements: Piso for Coughs and Colds, the Overland automobile. What about that oath I took in 1911?

At the Charleston Navy Yard in 1917. The admiral on the left is me.

I ignored the roaring twenties—gangsters, speakeasies, bathtub gin . . . and painted nostalgic subjects; a boy and his dog, the rube and the phrenologist.

In 1930, millionaires, grocery boys, dogs, and widows all watched the stock-exchange quotations.

1920–25	While plugging away at covers, ads, and illustrations, I find time for trips to Europe and South America.
1926	I paint the first *Post* cover ever reproduced in full color.
1927–28	I join the country club, play golf, join the beach club. Night life and parties. Sophistication. Two gay trips to Europe. I'm neglecting my work, and it shows.
1929	Crash! Divorce.
1930–31	I marry Mary Barstow. I resign from the country club and beach club, drop the night life and parties, and get back to work. My whole way of life changes. My first son, Jerry, is born.
1932–36	I have trouble with my work, spend eight futile months in France, experimenting with techniques. I finally readjust. Sons Tom and Peter arrive.
1939	We move to a farm in Arlington, Vermont. My neighbors are wonderful new models. Vermont is inspiration to my work.

I was pretty impressed with myself in 1934.

Mary and I leaving the marriage-license bureau.

1942	Great news! Ben Hibbs becomes editor-in-chief of the *Post;* Bob Fuoss becomes managing editor. I wake up at 2:00 A.M. wildly inspired: I'll illustrate the lofty Four Freedoms Proclamation of President Roosevelt in terms of the common man. I spend ten months painting the Four Freedoms.
1943	The *Post* features the Four Freedoms. My studio burns to the ground. We move down river to West Arlington.
1945	Ken Stuart becomes art editor. Hurrah!
1946	No more war covers. I go back to painting my neighbors and their doings.
1952	I dash to Denver to paint Mr. Eisenhower for the election cover.
1953	We move to Stockbridge, Massachusetts. A whole new set of models. I have my studio over Mr. Sullivan's meat market on Main Street.

Rough sketch of Main Street, Stockbridge, Massachusetts.

My home and studio in West Arlington, Vermont, 1945. Painting by Gene Pelham.

My three sons:

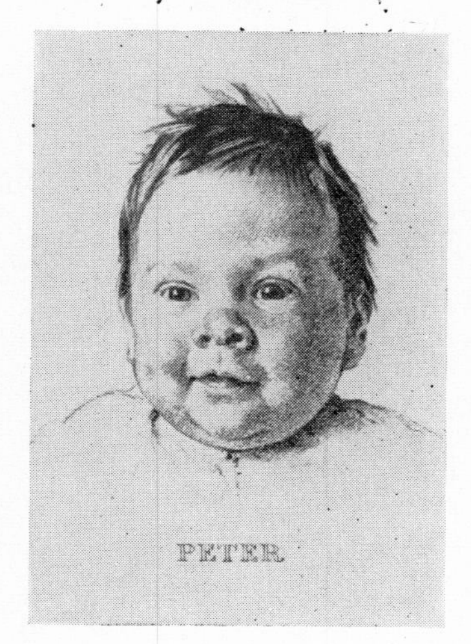

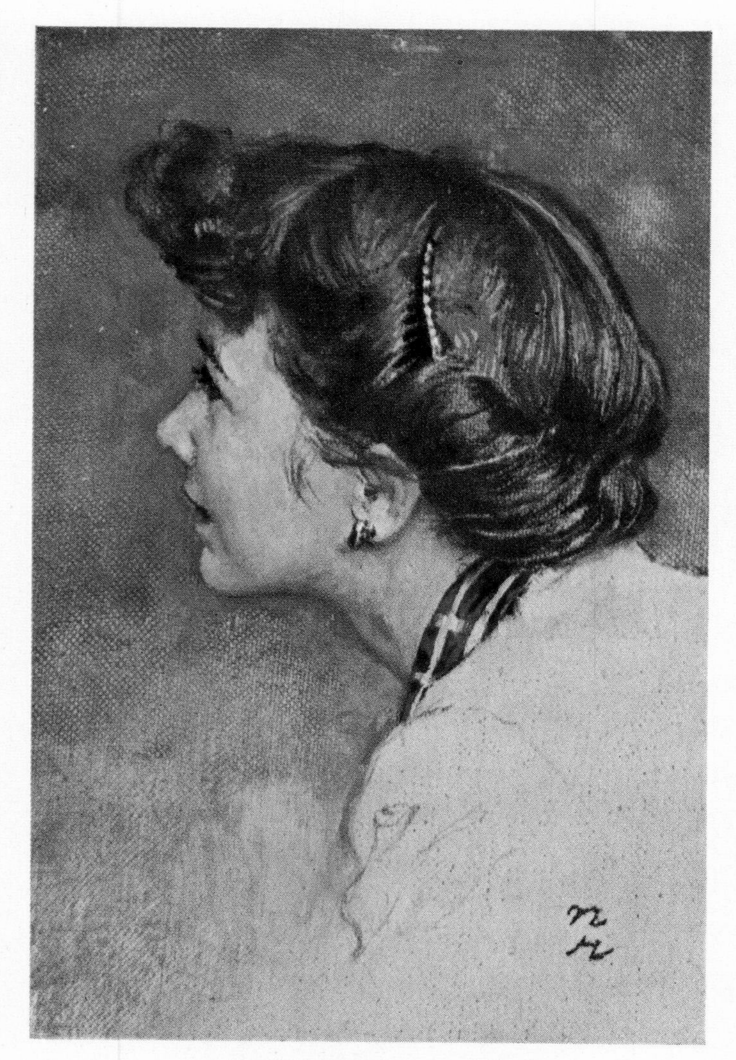

Mary Barstow Rockwell

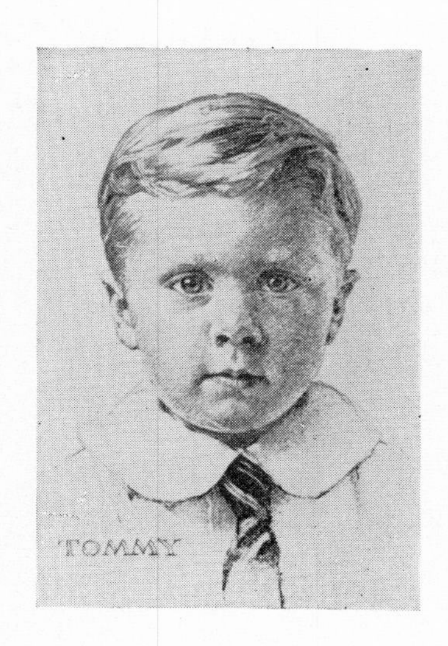

1956 Portraits of the candidates: Eisenhower and Stevenson.

1957 I buy an old house here in Stockbridge and remodel the carriage house into my best studio yet.

1959 My wife Mary dies.

1960 Portraits of the candidates again.

1961 Here I am, still painting.

EARLY ILLUSTRATIONS

In 1911, when I was seventeen years old, I illustrated a children's book entitled *Tell Me Why Stories*. It was my first job in illustration, and I worked hard on it. I was not satisfied with the finished paintings, but I was pleased with them. Looking at them now, I am amused. They are naïve, amateurishly conceived, crudely executed. But the publishers accepted them, and when I showed reproductions of them to the art editors of young people's magazines, I was assigned stories to illustrate.

But a great deal of the illustration of those days was crude, naïve, rather amateurish. There were many fine illustrators—Howard Pyle, Frederic Remington, Maxfield Parrish, A. B. Frost, Edwin Austin Abbey, Charles Dana Gibson—but, as in all periods, they were the exceptions, and their work was not representative of the general run of illustration. And at that time almost all the pictorial matter in magazines was illustration; very few photographs were used.

At first I worked almost exclusively for young people's magazines—*Boys' Life, St. Nicholas, Youths' Companion, Everyland, American Boy, Harper's Young People.* (*Boys' Life* is the only one still published: radio and the movies killed the rest; television buried them.) The stories I illustrated were about young people: Horatio Alger success stories, sports stories, adventure stories. For five or six years I painted nothing but kids. When, following my first *Post* cover in 1916, I began to do work for adult magazines, I continued to use kids as my principal subject matter. But now I looked at them in a different way. While working for the young people's magazines, I had portrayed kids from what I imagined was their viewpoint. I had treated their activities and concerns seriously, almost humorlessly, with the grave romanticism in over-all conception and the strict realism in details which I thought characterized their view of themselves. But now I attempted to amuse adults with the antics of kids or evoke nostalgia for the carefree pleasures of childhood. I painted them from that adult viewpoint, which sees childhood as a carefree, cute, blissful, uncomplicated, undemanding period — its sorrows, unimportant, transient; its pleasures, manifold. For the young people's magazines I had painted Frank Merriwell; for the adult magazines I painted Peck's Bad Boy.

A copy by my father of a drawing by George Henry Boughton. My father used occasionally to copy drawings from magazines for his own amusement. I never knew him to attempt any original work, and I am certain he had no artistic ambitions. He worked all his life for George Wood, Sons & Company, cotton brokers, rising from office boy to manager of the New York office. When I announced my intention of becoming an illustrator, he objected mildly. In those days art was not considered a particularly respectable profession. My mother, whose father had been an impoverished artist, a painter of portraits and landscapes by preference, occasionally a house painter by necessity, concurred. She had disliked her father because he mistreated her mother, drank heavily, and earned little. I suppose she extended her dislike to include her father's profession. But I don't remember that there was any determined opposition to my ambitions. My Aunt Kate used to claim that she had persuaded my parents to permit me to leave high school to enter art school. I doubt it. My parents let my brother Jarvis and me do pretty much as we wished. My father thought we ought to manage our own affairs. I earned my own tuition to art school and was self-supporting by the time I was seventeen years old.

I only wish I had one of
Frederic Remington's
early Western subjects.

One of Edwin Austin Abbey's Shakespearean illustrations.

A. B. Frost gave me this drawing
when he was a very old man.

A drawing by my hero of heroes: Howard Pyle.

Examples, from my collection, of the work of the great American illustrators of the Golden Age of Illustration. Their work influenced me while I was in art school, and still does.

Maxfield Parrish is ninety years old and still painting.

In 1914 most illustrations were reproduced in black and white. We painted with "illustrators' black," which is really a brown, so that the paintings wouldn't look funereal.

My mother boasted of her descent from the English Percevels and insisted that I sign my name N. *P.* Rockwell. But I hated the name Percevel and, when I left home, dropped the P.

One of the illustrations from a children's book entitled *Tell Me Why Stories*, my first job (it looks it) in illustration.

The boy telegrapher. As I remember, this was about the best of the many illustrations I did for the young people's magazines. I know I was terribly proud of it at the time. I'm not ashamed of it now.

An early attempt at humor. About the only subject which an illustrator for young people's magazines was permitted to treat humorously was rich, sissyish kids. The readers all identified with the regular fellows behind the car and laughed with them at the conceited, pompous sissy.

Shot down by blackhearted rustlers. I knew nothing about cowboys or gunplay. But I had not found myself yet, and eagerly painted any subject assigned me.

With the exception of *Life*, all the magazines whose covers are reproduced on these two pages are no longer being published. I hope it wasn't my fault. *Life*, of course, is no longer a humor magazine.

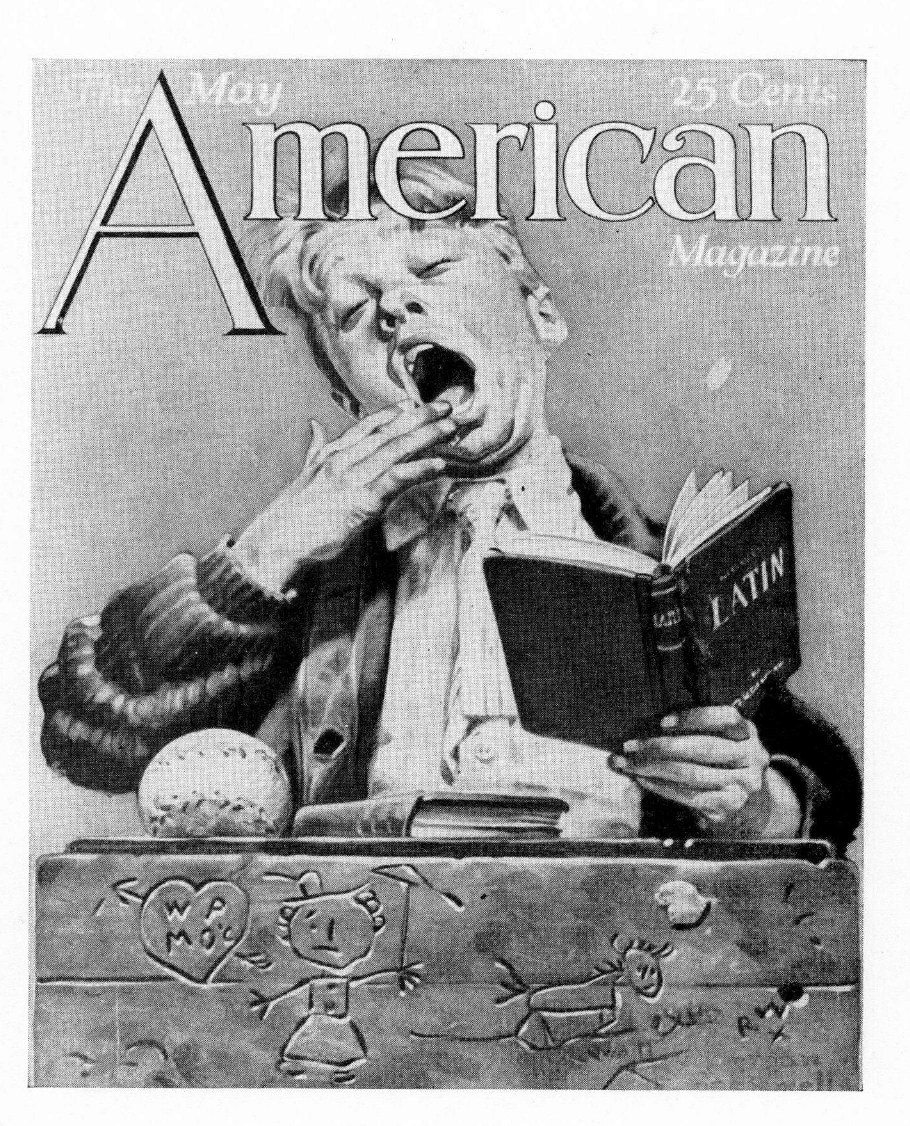

The Music Master

The *Country Gentleman* cover was one of a series I painted of the adventures of two rough-and-tumble kids, Fatty and Red, and a rich, prim sissy, Reginald Claude Fitzhugh. Fatty and Red were always getting the better of Reginald.

An early Thanksgiving Day cover for *Life*.

"Over There"—a *Life* cover painted during World War I.

One of several covers I did for *Popular Science*.

An early cover for *The Literary Digest*.

POST COVERS

My first cover for *The Saturday Evening POST*, published May 20, 1916.

My first election cover, painted in 1920. This is an example of the topical cover, in which I hope to catch the public's eye by depicting some current event or craze everybody is talking about.

I was a skinny kid with stringy arms and chicken legs myself. I lifted weights. It did no good. I was miserable. But years later I got a cover idea out of it.

An early cover, 1917. Another example of the topical cover, but a rather oblique one, for after five years of working for kids' magazines, I saw every subject in terms of kids, even an adult subject like this one: enlisting in the Army.

If one wants to paint covers for the *Post*, one must begin by accepting certain limitations. The cover must please a vast number of people (no matter how: by amusing, edifying, praising; but it *must* please); it must not require an explanation or caption to be understood; it must have an instantaneous impact (people won't bother to puzzle out a cover's meaning). These limitations might be stifling to some. They aren't to me. I guess I just naturally paint pictures which conform to them. And then, of course, there is nothing to prevent an illustrator from attempting to transcend them. I have always felt that a cover which provoked *only* an instantaneous reaction was a failure. A cover should do more; it should be more than just a one-line joke. I like to think that each time people look at one of my covers, they will see something new, something they had not noticed before, which will give the cover added meaning.

These limitations haven't changed at all since 1916, when I painted my first *Post* cover. But the subject matter of my covers has. Most of my early covers were of kids. Then, gradually, I began to paint situations involving adults. Many of these were costume pictures or, at least, pictures reflecting a nostalgia for nineteenth-century rural America, the world of *Tom Sawyer*. I did quite a few fanciful covers: "Springtime"—a boy playing a flute while little animals dance at his feet. Occasionally I painted a topical cover, usually some fad or craze (the ouija board in 1920), or something new (the crystal set in 1922), or an event of overwhelming public interest (Lindbergh's flight). Then, during the thirties, I sensed that people were no longer enjoying nostalgic pictures. Evidently the contemporary scene was too exciting and too anxious—the depression, communism, fascism, war—people no longer had time for nostalgia. I began to concentrate on contemporary life. My last costume picture dates from 1939. War came. I painted the home front in wartime. Since the war I have found my cover ideas in the everyday lives of my neighbors. And sometimes I have tried to give my work a deeper significance by commenting on some of the more serious aspects of life.

We viewed the wonders of the world through the stereoscope when I was young.

Before 1926, *Post* covers were printed in two colors only, red and black. It is amazing what you can do with only two colors. Still, it was sort of frustrating. I often used more colors just to make the original look better. I remember I painted the violinist's coat rusty green.

Thinking up ideas for *Post* covers is difficult. I don't remember where I got the barbershop quartet, but the other came out of my own youth. I had an uncle who used to come to visit us, his pockets stuffed with gifts.

The first *Post* cover printed in full color, published in 1926. I chose the colonial sign painter as my subject for this cover because I thought it would give me an opportunity to use as many different colors as possible.

My model for the burly fellow was Pop Fredericks, an old actor who moaned he had been cheated of fame. The great actors, he said, had always been jealous and cut his lines.

I painted James K. Van Brunt, who posed for this cover, many times. I couldn't resist that bushy mustache, which measured eight full inches from tip to tip.

I loved to do costume pictures. Modern clothes are rather meager, drab, and boring; costumes are picturesque and colorful.

A fanciful cover. The model's name, rather appropriately, was Eric Nightingale.

An example of the human-interest cover, which depicts with gentle humor the everyday foibles of people like ourselves.

Before I began to paint from photographs of my models children were a problem. They won't hold still; they fidget. But it customarily took me two days to paint a figure working from the model. So I used to make quick sketches of the kids, working fast and furiously. The sketch above right, is one of many I made of the little girl. As you can see, it is not the one I used.

Meeting deadlines and thinking up ideas are the scourges of an illustrator's life. This is not a caricature of myself; I really look like that.

Painting pretty girls has never been my strong point. I don't really know why.

The model for the sheriff was Harvey McKee, an undersheriff in Arlington, Vermont. He was tough but sentimental.

The Chicago & North-Western railroad station in Chicago at Christmastime, 1944. Most of the people were actual travelers. I stood on the announcer's balcony and directed a photographer on the floor of the station.

The rough sketch and the final cover. The original now hangs in the Baseball Hall of Fame at Cooperstown.

Some favorite subjects (1925–34): Santa Claus, kids, and picturesque old men.

A typical assortment of models: Gary Cooper as the cowboy actor; James K. Van Brunt, minus his mustache, as two of the old gossips (I couldn't find an old lady funny-looking enough); Dave Campion, the local druggist, as the traffic cop; a little girl.

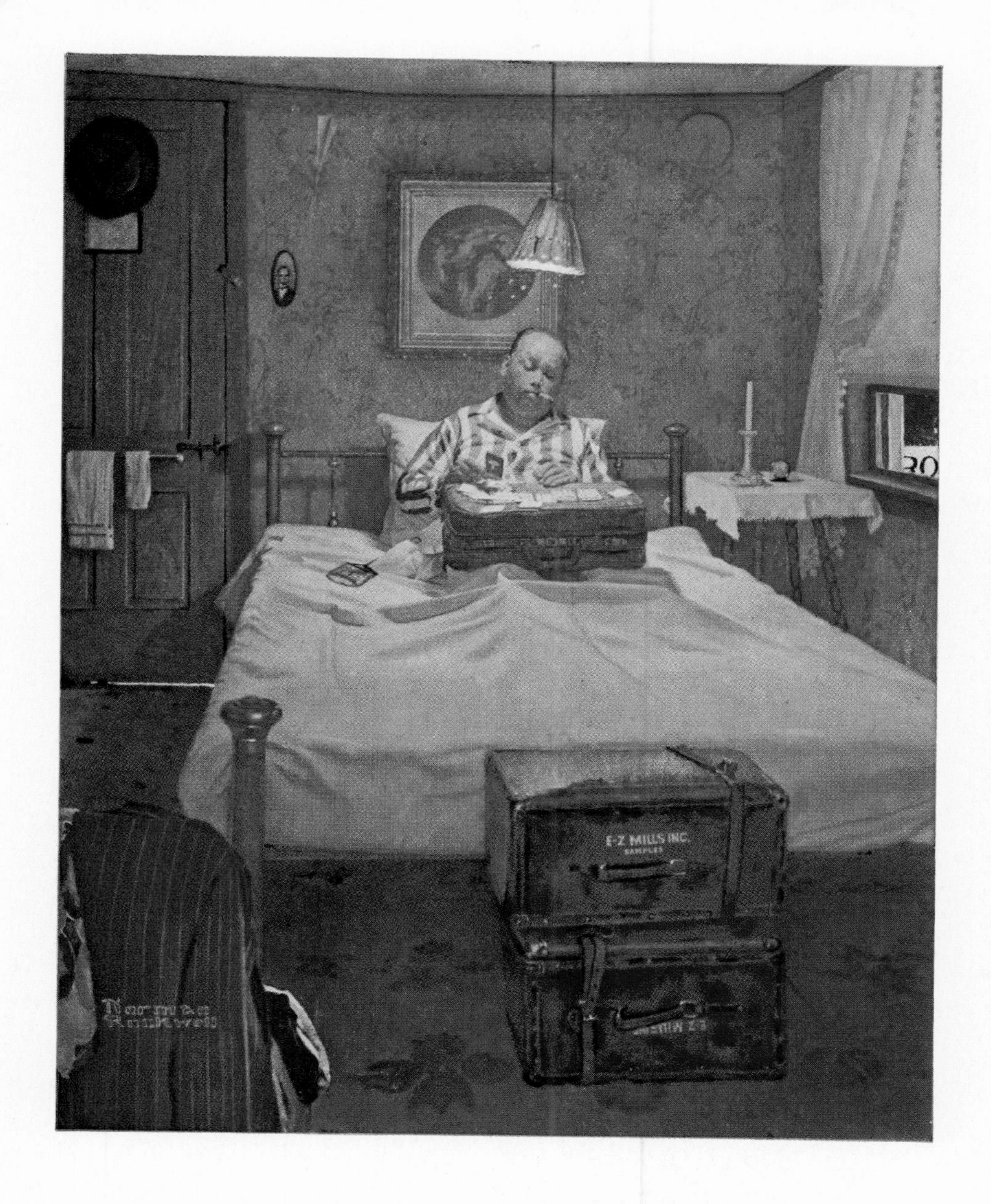

Traveling salesmen don't lead a gay, roistering life; the old traveling-salesman-farmer's-daughter stories give a false impression. I've known a few traveling salesmen; they lead a pretty lonely life. That's what I was trying to express in this cover.

Figuring out the tip is a problem to everybody. It certainly is to me. Some people say 10 per cent; the more affluent say 20 per cent. But when it comes to a youngster, like my son Peter, who posed for the boy, it is a real puzzle, even under the kindly eye of a benevolent waiter.

Pop Fredericks, the old actor, posed for the doctor. He was a man of many parts. I used him as a model for (among others) a thug, Mr. Pickwick, Benjamin Franklin, a cellist, Santa Claus, an actor, a hobo, a tourist, a pompous politician, a piccoloist, and a Christmas reveler.

Following the publication of this cover, I received many letters from schoolteachers complaining bitterly that I had insulted them. Schoolteachers were not drab, funny-looking old maids. I still don't understand why a picture of one old-maid schoolteacher implies that I think *all* schoolteachers are drab old maids.

I don't have an especially good memory, but whenever I look at one of my *Post* covers, even an early one, I remember all the troubles I had with it, the models' names, where it was painted, the state of my health while I was painting it, the technique I used, where I got the props and costumes—everything, in fact, which was in any way related to it. I can remember, for instance, that Pop Fredericks, the model for Mr. Pickwick, posed in long woolen underwear and vest, that I had trouble painting the pitcher in the "Hundredth Year of Baseball" cover, that the cover of the kids playing marbles was the first one I painted in Arlington, Vermont, that I had to bribe my son Tommy, who posed as the boy reading his sister's diary, to stop fidgeting and sit still.

MUGGLETON
STAGE COACH

Norman
Rockwell

Telling a son the facts of life is always a problem to a father. When I was a boy, my father purchased a set of books entitled *What a Boy Should Know at Ten*, *What a Boy Should Know at Eleven*, and so on. He hid the books, but my brother and I found them and had already read the book for seventeen-year-olds while my father was still struggling to explain the one for ten-year-olds.

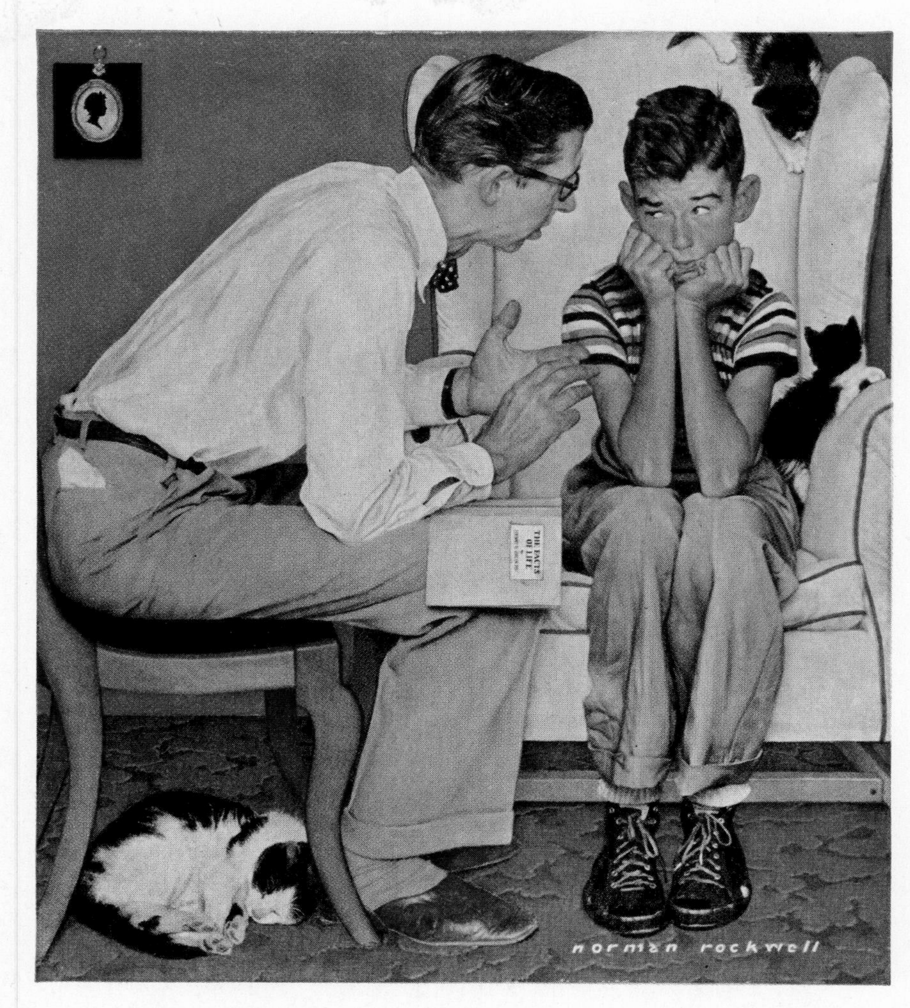

"A Day in a Boy's Life." I later painted "A Day in a Girl's Life," but it wasn't as good or as popular, I guess because a little boy leads a more active and varied life than a little girl.

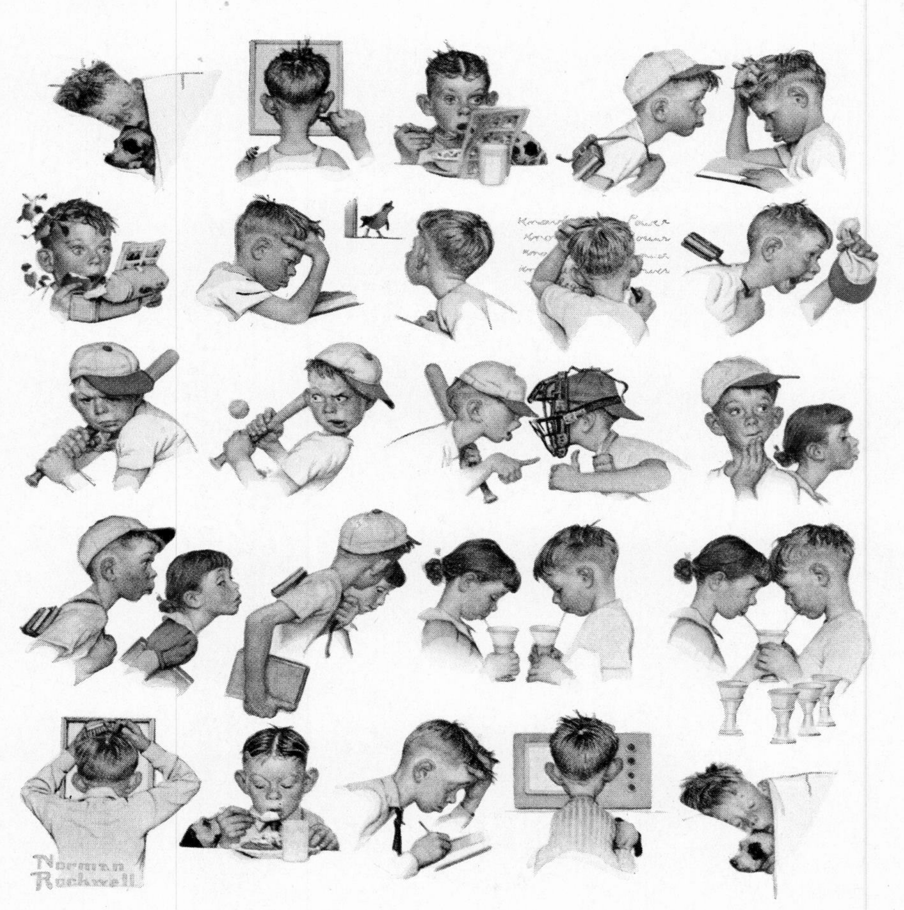

The census taker's book is entitled *California*. People wrote from there to inquire what that strange, long, sticklike thing at his feet was used for.

I receive many letters noting mistakes in my covers. I always apologize for the mistake, though sometimes it wasn't a mistake at all. In 1943, after twenty-seven years of this, I painted an April Fool cover which I deliberately loaded with forty-five mistakes and incongruities. But you can't win. A man wrote claiming to have found one hundred and twenty.

My second April Fool cover.

My third and last April Fool cover.

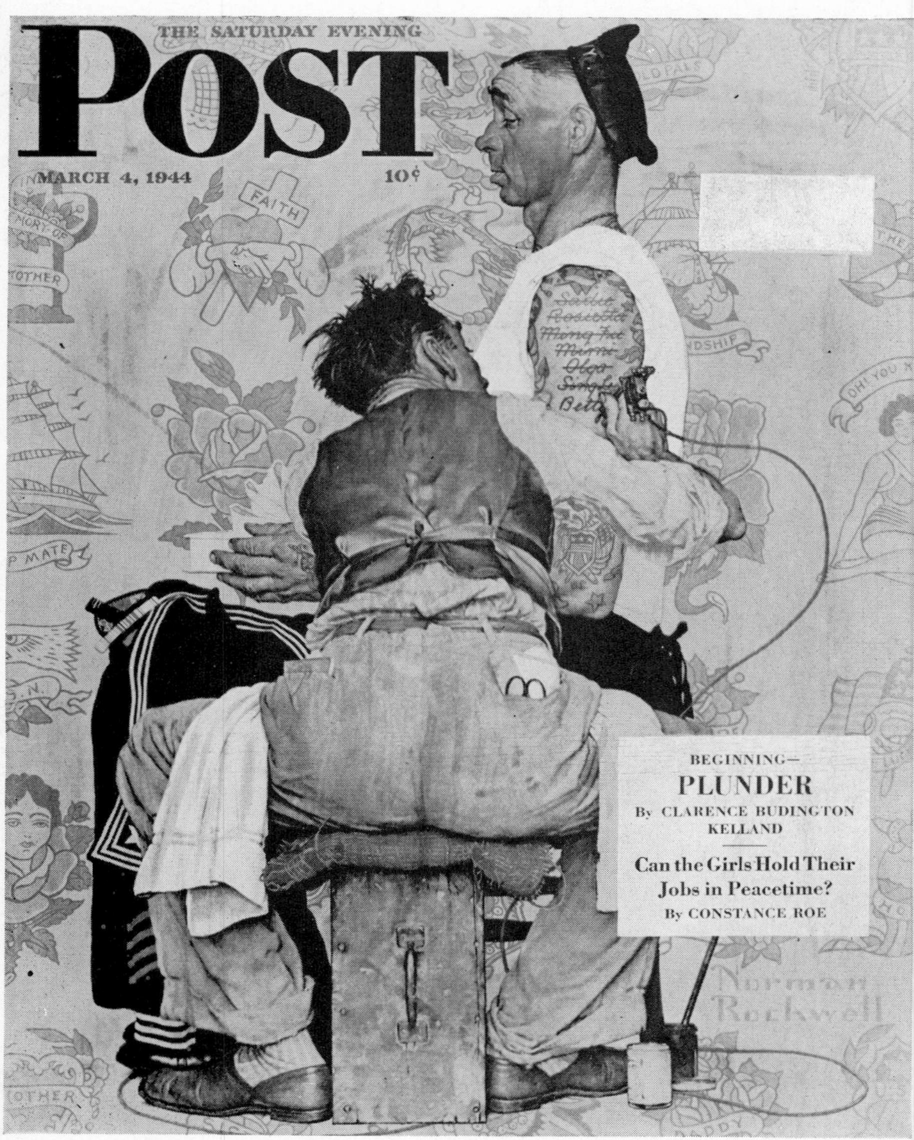

I needed to know what sort of equipment a tattooer used. Behind a ragged curtain in a dark, dirty corner in the rear of a combination pool hall, barbershop, and restaurant in the Bowery I found a tattooer. I had been toying with the idea of getting a small tattoo myself, but the greasy state of his instruments and his smudged hands dissuaded me.

James K. Van Brunt, who posed for the druggist, was a veteran of the Civil War, the Indian wars on the Western plains, and the Spanish-American War, and claimed to be the same height as Napoleon. He was terribly upset when the Army refused his services during World War I.

The first and last covers in my Willie Gillis series, painted during World War II, depicting the adventures of a draftee, an innocent little fellow, in the strange, new world of the Army.

A peculiar case. In a junkshop one day I discovered the fancy fireman's frame which appears in this cover. It was empty. I felt I had to fill it. So I painted this cover, using the frame, and then put the painting in the frame. So, you see, the frame's in the picture, and the picture's in the frame.

It is possible to fake a setting, but it is never entirely satisfactory. A concocted setting is bound to lack authenticity; some little detail which would make the painting ring true will be missing. So, whenever possible, I like to visit and photograph or make sketches of the actual setting of a cover. The room in this cover is an exact reproduction of the model's own room, from the skates and pajamas hanging on the closet door to the old piano stool.

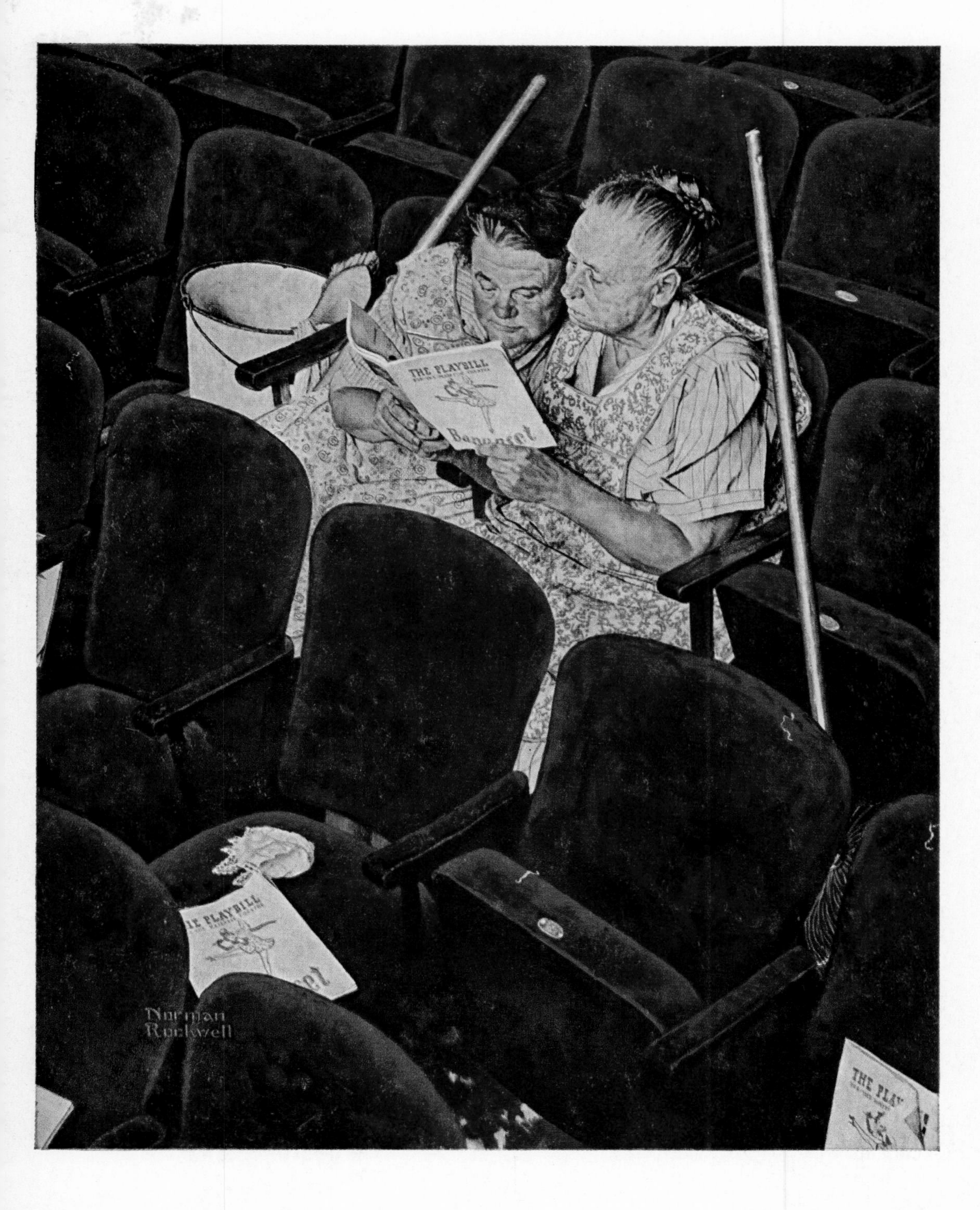

Two of my neighbors in Arlington posed as the charwomen. They were very respected and respectable ladies and at first balked at posing as charwomen. But I convinced them that they were only acting; no one would think the worse of them for it; an actress wasn't considered a murderess because she had played Lady Macbeth. I've run into this attitude a number of times. Once I portrayed a high-toned society matron as a portly maid; she never spoke to me again.

I like to do a picture which, instead of depicting a single incident or a single moment in time, traces the course of an action over a period of time. Here one can see that the salesman got out of his car, took off his clothes but not his shoes (his feet are tender), spread a newspaper on the grass and laid his glasses on it; then, at the water's edge, took off his shoes, waded in, and, just before submerging, carefully laid his lighted cigar on his shoe, ready to be puffed the minute he emerges from the stream.

This was the first of the two-part *Post* covers and I'm kind of proud that I painted it.

A topical cover, painted in 1949, heralding the advent of commercial television. In those days we weren't blasé about television; it was a wonder and a miracle.

FROM MY SKETCHBOOKS

Some illustrators feel that their commercial work is just a way of making a living—nothing more. Their serious painting, the painting by which they hope to be remembered and into which they pour their talents, ideas, and energies, they do in their spare time.

I don't feel that way. A *Post* cover, an ad, an illustration, is never just a check to me. It means a whole lot more than that. Whatever talents, energies, and ideas I have go into the painting of it. Consequently I rarely do anything but my regular work.

But occasionally I get to feeling that I'm in a rut, I'm tightening up, my work is not improving, I'd like to be slapdash and experimental. But one can't do that on a commercial job to any extent. It has to be acceptable to the client, conform to certain requirements. So I hire a model and do some sketching, or join a sketch class, or go off on a trip with my sketchbook—but never with the idea of giving up my regular work, always with the hope of improving it, of shaking myself up so that I will do a better *Post* cover.

I cannot really convince myself that any painting is good unless it is popular. If the public dislikes one of my *Post* covers, I can't help disliking it myself or, at least, doubting it. I am never sure whether or not a painting is good until I have heard the public's opinion of it. This is foolish. I know it. Popularity alone is never a measure of excellence. I should trust my own judgment. But it explains, in part, why I haven't done more painting and sketching on my own.

Pages from a sketchbook. FRANCE, 1932.

chapeaux
bijouterie
cafe
Rue Vaugirard
Paris
coiffeur
de tabac

Lanterne
Senlis

Chateau
Fontainbleu
april
Pont Neuf
Paris april '32

La cour du
Grand-Cerf
Orry-la-ville

Senlis
gargoyle Saint Pierre.
sign over mustard shop

sunshine
rain
The Canal
Fontainebleau
April 9.

Gray-la-ville
7/20/32
le chateau
Comtesse Noëllay

Around the World in 1958.

The route of my trip around the world for Pan American World Airways.

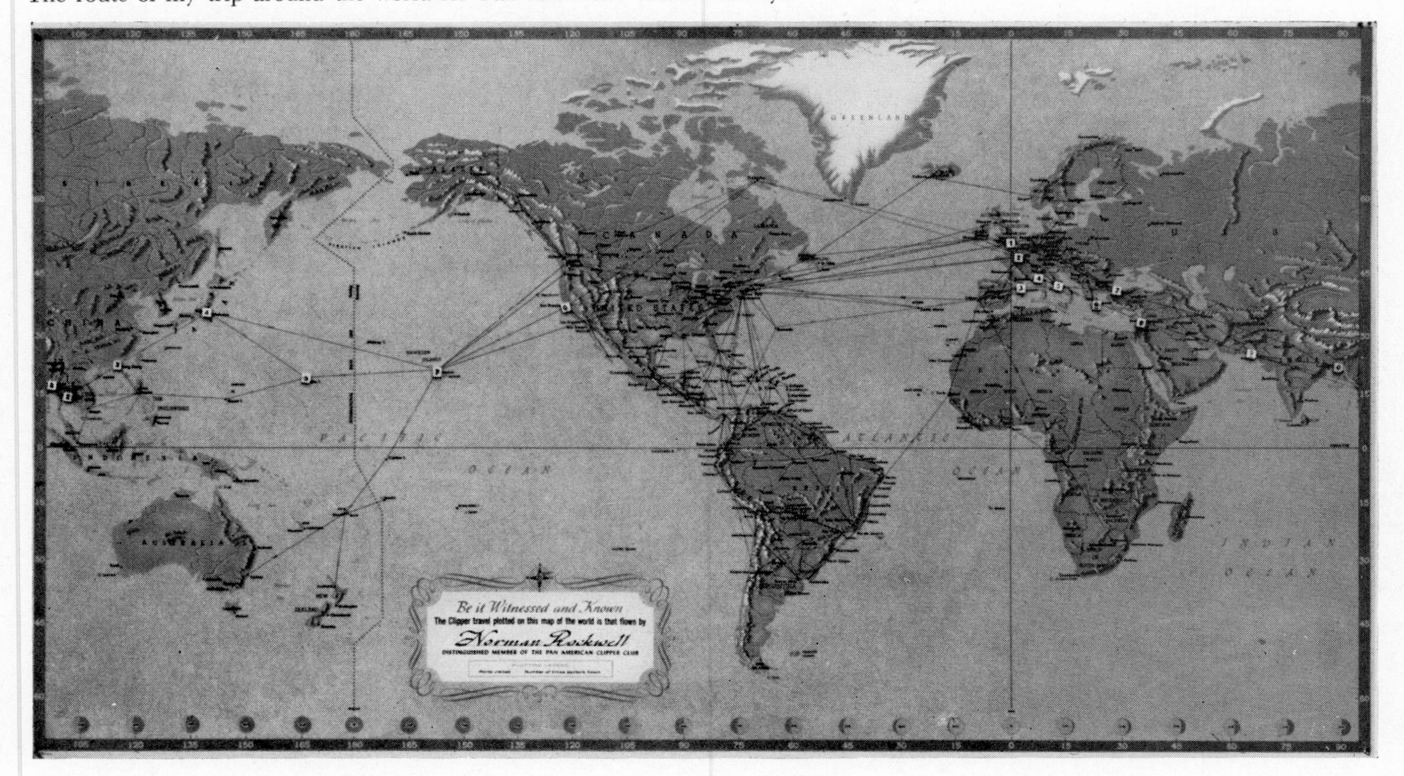

ENGLAND.

Which way to the hotel?

FRANCE.

SPAIN.

ITALY.

TURKEY AND LEBANON.

Benaras
India
magician
Snake charmer
bed of thorns
soothsayer
monkey trainer

INDIA.

THAILAND.

HONG KONG.

JAPAN.

HAWAII . . . then San Francisco and home. A wonderful adventure.

HOLLAND: spring, 1960.

SKETCH CLASS

A sketch in oils of the sketch class which meets every Thursday morning at the studio of Peggy Worthington Best here in Stockbridge.

We begin about nine-thirty and work until noon. The model poses for twenty minutes, then rests for ten. Sometimes the model assumes four or five different poses during a morning, at other times only one pose. There is a different model each week. One doesn't have time to do a finished portrait, but that's all to the good as far as I'm concerned. I have a tendency to overwork a painting. In sketch class I can't do that. There isn't time for more than a sketch. The portrait of the old woman took me about two and a half hours; the oil sketch of the reclining woman, about twenty minutes.

I experiment with mediums, techniques, and materials in sketch class, something I can't do to any great extent in my regular work. The girl and satyr is oil on canvas; the sketch of the seated man on this page and the one of the man's head on the opposite page were done with a quill pen and India ink. The young man crowned with a halo was painted in casein and oil. The sketch of the girl's head on the opposite page was done in oil on a sheet of rice paper.

Sometimes I get kind of playful in sketch class. I indulge my fancy. Note the leering satyr in the portrait of the girl on the facing page and the halo over the young man's head. It's fun and loosens me up.

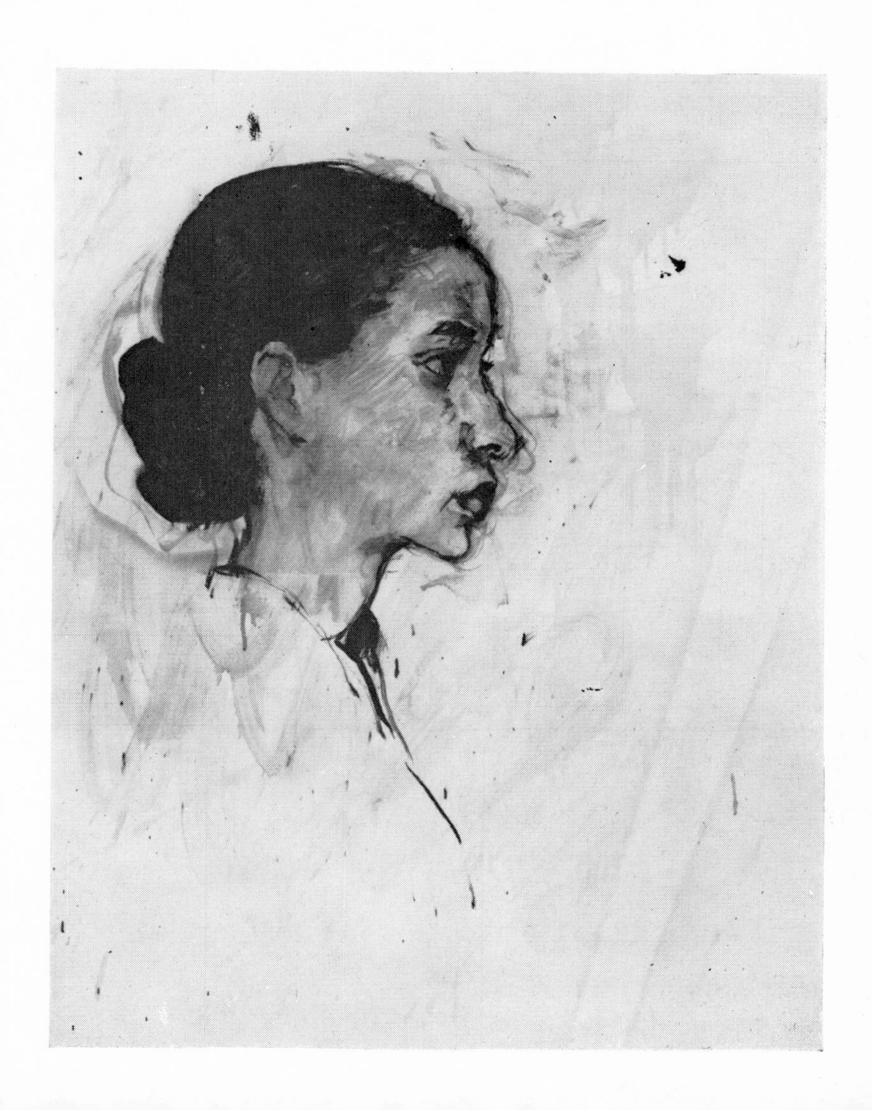

Some mornings I lay the canvas on the floor and paint kneeling. I paint with large brushes; I paint with a palette knife. Anything to break my regular working habits. . . . It took me about twenty minutes to paint each of the three sketches of the girl reproduced above (I spent another fifteen minutes on the one in the center before deciding to rub it out). After each rest period I turned the canvas around and moved my easel so that I had a different view of the model.

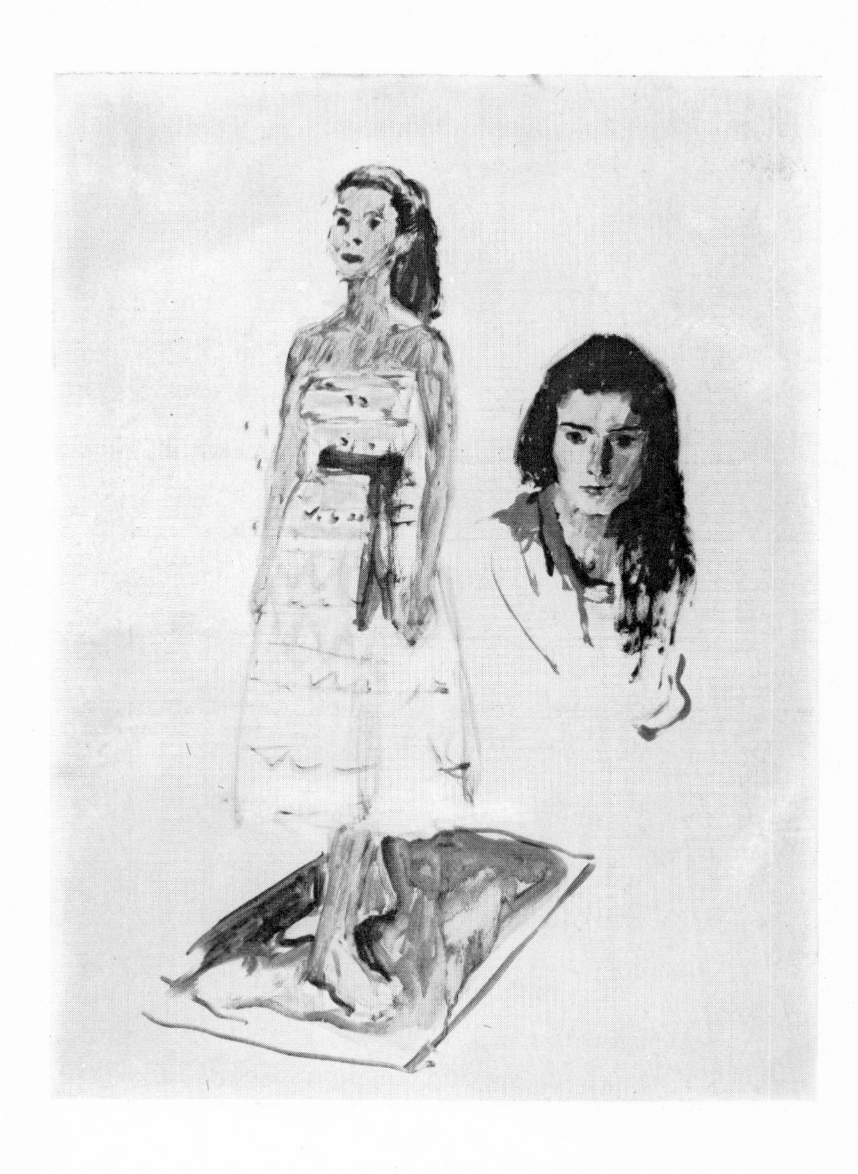

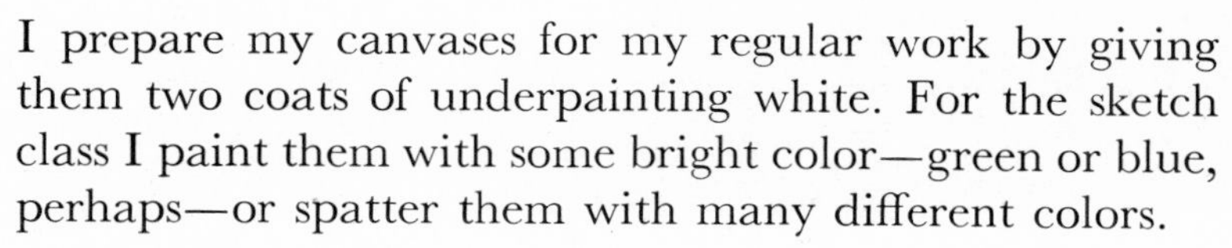

I prepare my canvases for my regular work by giving them two coats of underpainting white. For the sketch class I paint them with some bright color—green or blue, perhaps—or spatter them with many different colors.

The drawing above and the portrait to the left were not done in the Thursday sketch class. The portrait, painted on burlap, was an experiment in glazing. I made the drawing some years ago in Vermont.

Dwight Eisenhower. Denver, 1952

Mamie Eisenhower. 1952

PRESIDENTS AND CANDIDATES

DWIGHT D. EISENHOWER

After a call from the *Post*, I flew out to Denver. A two-and-a-half-hour appointment with Mr. Eisenhower had been arranged. I was extremely nervous. But Mr. Eisenhower put me at my ease immediately. He has more personal charm than any other man I have ever met. While I sketched him, we chatted about fishing and painting. I must have acted rather flurried, because he told me not to hurry, he wasn't going fishing until that afternoon. His face is wonderfully mobile, the range of expression amazing. I asked him to assume about every expression I could think of; I wanted to be sure to get everything I'd need for the portrait. He barked a drill command, looked worried, laughed. Then I asked for a pleasant expression, suggesting that he think about something that he liked, saying I told kids to think about ice cream. He remarked that he had some pretty nice grandchildren, and his eyes sparkled, his face seemed to glow.

Norman
Rockwell

ADLAI E. STEVENSON

It was July and brutally hot. A magazine photographer was posing Mr. Stevenson perched on a fence rail wearing a straw hat and sucking a blade of grass. Mr. Stevenson looked uncomfortable — as much from the unnatural folksy pose, I judged, as from the heat. He entered the house, perspiring and weary, and went upstairs to change his shirt. When he returned, I said I didn't want a folksy pose; would he just look pleasant? He seemed relieved. After the photographs had been taken and I'd made a quick color sketch, we sat on the patio and chatted. I said I would vote for him if he would make Chester Bowles his Secretary of State. He laughed affably.

Norman
Rockwell

RICHARD M. NIXON

The Senate was in session. Mr. Nixon, as presiding officer, had to attend. I was told I could have forty-five minutes with him. A Secret Service man entered, then Mr. Nixon. In photographs he looks rather dark-complexioned and grim. In person this impression is contradicted by his ruddy complexion and the grave animation of his face. Photographs were taken of Mr. Nixon and a Congressman for the latter's home-town newspaper. Mr. Nixon talked knowledgeably with the Congressman about his district. As I was posing him, Mr. Nixon remarked that he had a hard face to paint. I demurred. But while painting the portrait, I found it difficult to render my impression of him, for so much of his charm arises from his vigorous smile and his smooth, abrupt, warm manner.

Norman
Rockwell

JOHN F. KENNEDY

It was a cold, misty morning in Hyannis Port. Mr. Kennedy leaned out of an upstairs window in his pajamas and said to go right on into the house, he would be down in a minute. While Mr. Kennedy ate his breakfast, I selected a room in which to take the photographs. As I posed him, I remarked that I thought a rather dignified, serious pose would be best; his youthful appearance should not be emphasized. He agreed. Afterward we walked out to the breakwater near the house to see his sailboat. As we were returning to the house, Mr. Kennedy suggested that we try the pose again. He felt that he had been a little stiff the first time. We did, and his expression was just what I had wanted — serious, with a certain dignity, but relaxed and pleasant, not hard.

Norman
Rockwell

Drawn two days after my first studio in Arlington burned in 1943.

ILLUSTRATIONS AND SO ON

When someone calls me a commercial artist, I cringe. The term seems to denote an artist who paints only because it pays, or, worse, an artist whose work has no other value than a commercial one; his work isn't a painting, it's a product, like an icebox, which, once worn out, is junked as valueless. I can't swallow that.

I prefer to be called an illustrator. But, though it lacks the repugnant connotations of "commercial artist," it really isn't a satisfactory term either, because it doesn't include the major portion of my work. *Post* covers are independent, storytelling pictures; they don't "illustrate" anything. Through the years I've done a great many paintings for advertisements. But these cannot be termed illustrations either. I did a series of pictorial reports for the *Post*: "Norman Rockwell Visits a Ration Board," "Norman Rockwell Visits a County Agent," and so on. Reports, not illustrations.

I suppose I could just call myself an artist, but that doesn't—well, it doesn't feel right. I can't say why. Maybe I want to have my humble pie and eat it too.

So I call myself an illustrator; it's the most comfortable term I can think of. And, of course, I have painted a great many illustrations.

I might call myself a cover artist. That's the work I enjoy most. And it's the most difficult. Illustrations are relatively easy; one's inspiration comes from the story or book. Advertisements don't require inspiration; they come off the top of your head. Reports are more difficult; you must find the story and then decide how to tell it. Still, the story exists independently of yourself; it doesn't have to be created.

But the term "cover artist" is even more exclusive than "illustrator." Besides, it's too close to "cover girl," and, while I am all for cover girls, the confusion would be embarrassing. I'm an "illustrator." I'm an "illustrator-and-so-on."

During the 1940s I did a series of pictorial reports for the *Post*, variously entitled "Norman Rockwell Visits a Country School," "Norman Rockwell Visits His Family Doctor," and so on. Each report consisted of a full-color painting, printed as a double-page spread, and two pages of black and white sketches done in Wolff pencil. I usually spent two days at the scene of the report. During the first day I tried to get the feel of the place and rough out in my mind the story I wanted to tell. The second day I made sketches, decided on the subject and setting of the painting, and had photographs taken. Back in my studio I did the painting and made the finished sketches. I enjoyed doing these reports. They were a pleasant and stimulating change from my regular work—*Post* covers, advertisements, illustrations—and gave me a chance to travel about the country and meet a lot of people.

Mrs. Effie McGuire reading to her pupils at Oak Mountain School.

The Oak Mountain School, a weatherbeaten clapboard building, sat atop a tall clay hill in Carroll County, Georgia. When I visited it, there were only forty pupils in attendance; some years, I was told, there were as many as seventy-five. Mrs. Effie McGuire, the wife of a farmer, taught all seven grades in the one room. The kids loved her. A Georgia educator told me: "She's an unusual teacher. She's able, through kindness, a quiet voice, and a love of children, to free their minds so they can learn."

I arrived at Oak Mountain School late one afternoon and discovered to my dismay that, in preparation for my visit, the children had come to school dressed in their best clothes—starched pinafores, bright calico dresses, neckties, jackets, shining yellow shoes. The girls smoothed down their dresses and looked pleased. The boys stuffed their hands in their pockets and looked uncomfortable. I explained to Mrs. McGuire that I wanted to report a typical day at Oak Mountain School, and she asked the children to wear their everyday clothes the next day. They did, and the change seemed to help them to overcome their shyness. They performed a dramatic skit, held a spelling bee, and went about their chores and studies perfectly naturally, almost as if I wasn't scurrying about, sketch pad in hand, and my photographer wasn't climbing on chairs to get a better angle. I think this report was the best of the series—not because of anything I did, but because of Mrs. Effie McGuire and her pupils.

Dr. George Russell in his office in Arlington. At the time this picture was painted, Dr. Russell had been physician, friend, and adviser to the townspeople for almost fifty years.

The rough sketch of the painting. Some people questioned the ethics of permitting a dog in the office, but nobody ever seemed the worse for it.

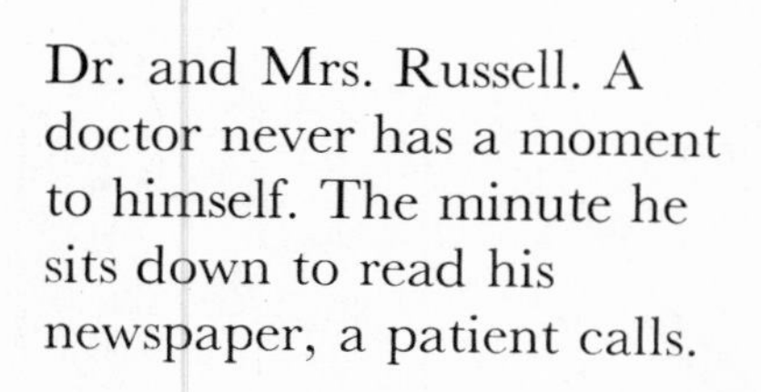

Dr. and Mrs. Russell. A doctor never has a moment to himself. The minute he sits down to read his newspaper, a patient calls.

Dr. Russell in his library. His collection of Vermontiana is one of the best in the state and is now housed in a special building erected by the townspeople as an affectionate tribute to Dr. Russell.

Dr. Russell was not deterred from making a call by rough dirt roads and nasty weather. He relaxed at his cabin in the woods, catching up on his reading or fishing in the mountain stream which ran close by.

The painting for the report of my visit with Herald K. Rippey, a county agricultural agent in Indiana.

The editorial offices of the *Monroe County Appeal* at Paris, Missouri. Jack Blanton, who was editor of the paper when this picture was painted, is seated at his typewriter. He was a charming old gentleman and known as one of the finest small-town newspaper editors in the country.

A sketch of the ancient linotype machine used by the *Monroe County Appeal*.

A detail from the painting reproduced above in black and white.

"The Ration Board"—in Manchester, Vermont. Painted in 1944.

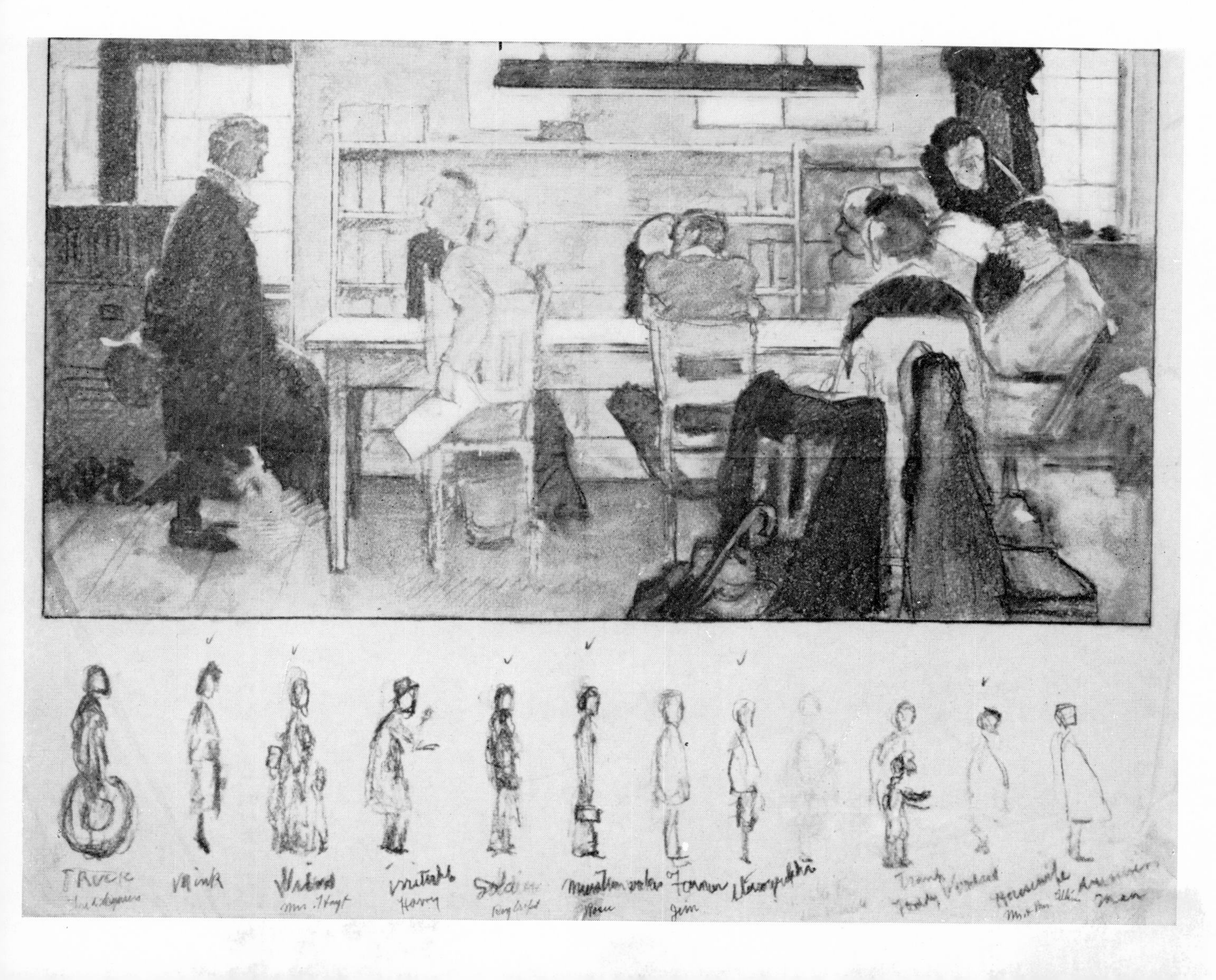

The rough sketch. The line of figures below the painting represents petitioners pleading their cases before the ration board. The scribbles under each figure are character notes and names of proposed models.

Illustrations for Mark Twain's
TOM SAWYER and HUCKLEBERRY FINN

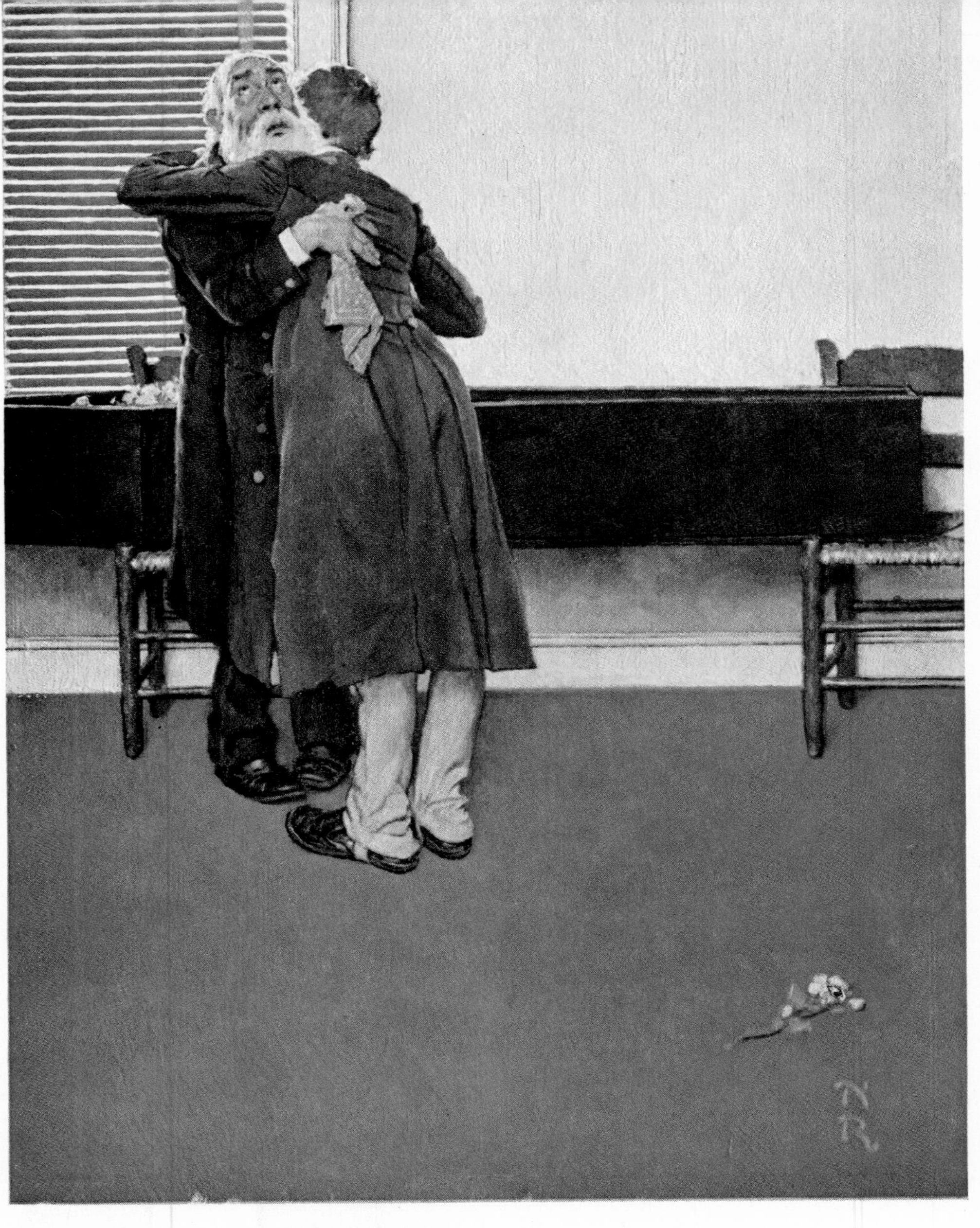

"Then for three minutes, or maybe four, I never see two men leak the way they done."
HUCKLEBERRY FINN

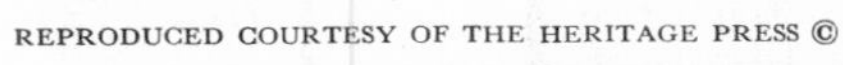

"Then Miss Watson took me in the closet and prayed but nothing come of it."
HUCKLEBERRY FINN

"The master's arm performed until it was tired and the stock of switches notably diminished." TOM SAWYER

"He spied the beetle; the drooping tail lifted and wagged." TOM SAWYER

"He meow'd with caution once or twice."
TOM SAWYER

"Both boys were looking very pale and miserable." TOM SAWYER

REPRODUCED COURTESY OF THE HERITAGE PRESS ©

"Well, I don't see why I oughtn't to like it. Does a boy get a chance to whitewash a fence every day?" TOM SAWYER

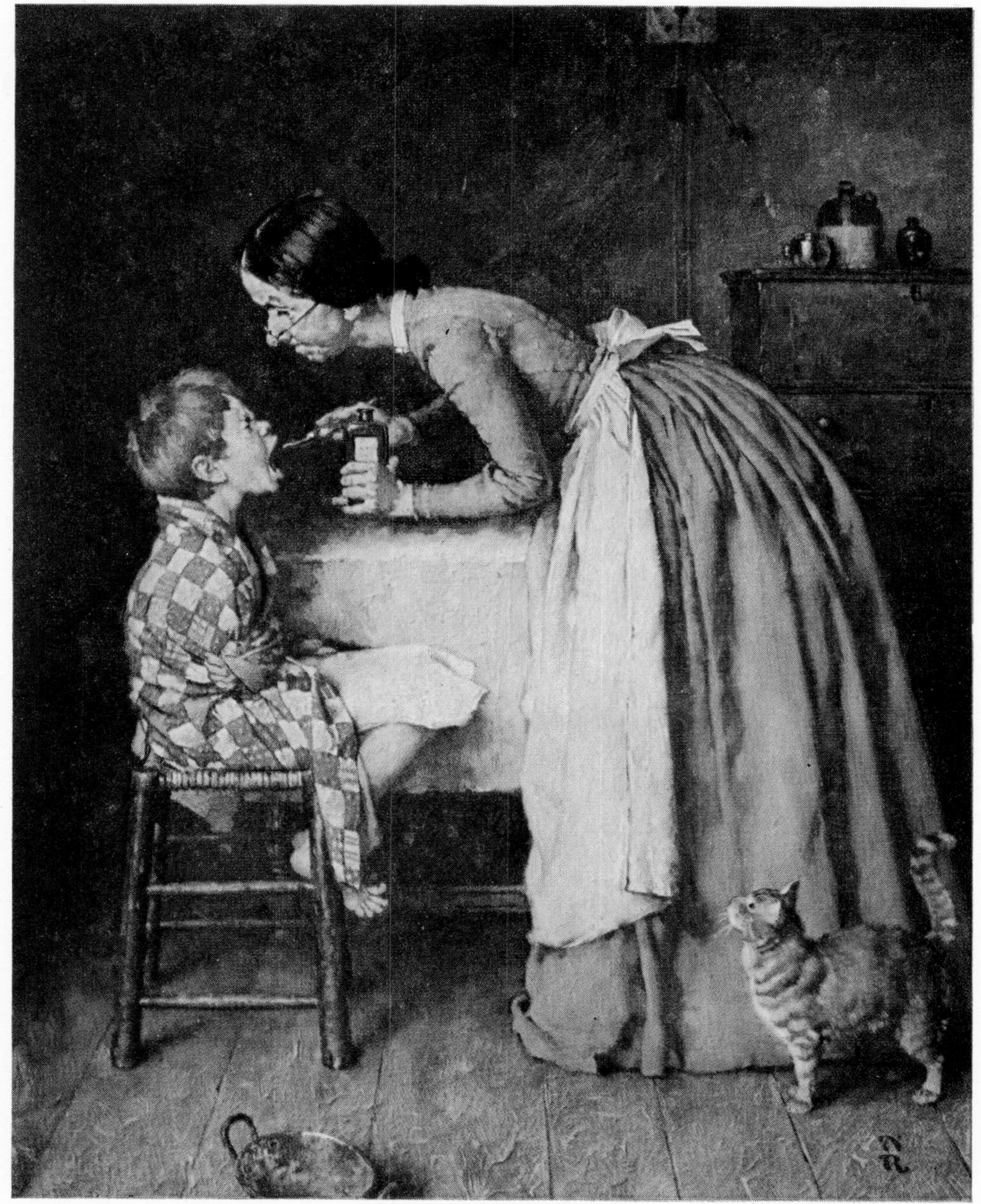

"She calculated his capacity as she would a jug's and filled him up every day with quack cure-alls." TOM SAWYER

Years ago I decided to do a series of pictures of the celebrated characters of American fiction. The series was to be published as a book, each picture accompanied by an excerpt from the work in which the character figured. I painted Ichabod Crane and Captain Ahab and then gave up the series, partly because I had lost interest in it and partly because I disliked the idea of a book of excerpts.

"Mr. Bhaer saw the drops on her cheeks; stooping down, he asked—'Heart's dearest, why do you cry?'" An illustration of a scene from Louisa May Alcott's *Little Women,* Chapter 46.

Louisa May Alcott being interviewed by her first publisher. An illustration for a biography of Louisa May Alcott published by the *Woman's Home Companion.*

The color sketch of an illustration for *The American Magazine.*

A portrait of Raymond Massey as Abraham Lincoln, done for the theater program of Robert Sherwood's *Abe Lincoln in Illinois.*

A detail from the painting reproduced above in black and white, an illustration painted in 1938 for a story about a little boy's visit with his grandparents in the country. I stopped doing illustrations nine or ten years ago, when the editors of the *Post* asked me to concentrate on painting covers.

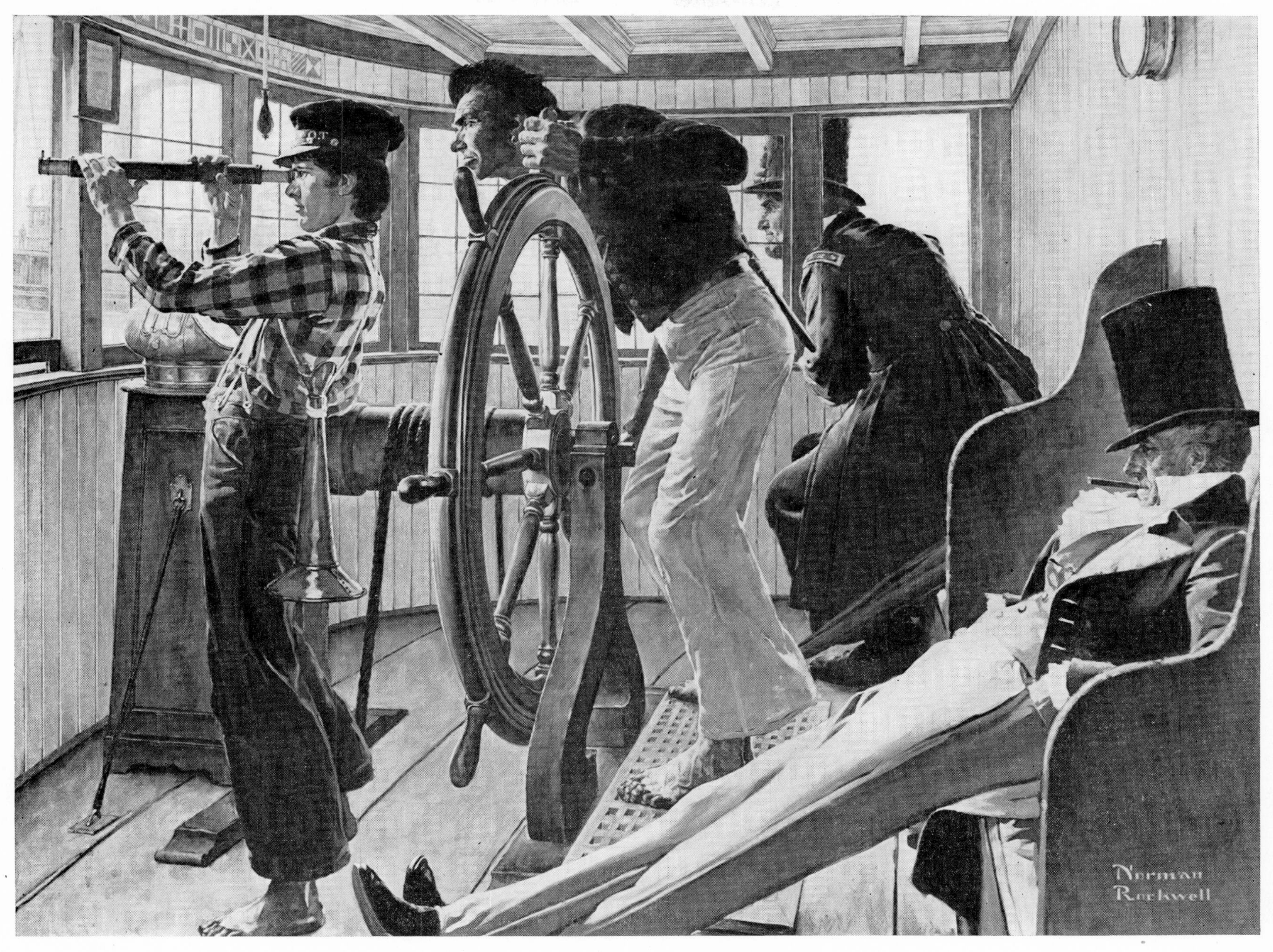

One of my better illustrations, I think. It was painted for a wonderful story about a race between two steamboats on the Connecticut River.

A Wolff-pencil drawing done for the cover of a history of Berkshire County, Massachusetts, 1761–1961. The right-hand section of the drawing was printed on the front cover; the left-hand section, on the back cover.

COURTESY THE BERKSHIRE EAGLE

The great horseshoe-forging contest. The drawing below depicts the crowd gathering to witness the contest. I always liked the wording of the sign outside the shop—"Practical and Artistic Horse Shoeing"—which I took verbatim from the sign outside Mr. Moon's blacksmith shop in South Shaftsbury, Vermont, where I did the research for this illustration.

Norman
Rockwell

COURTESY BROWN AND BIGELOW

I have painted a Boy Scout calendar every year for more than thirty-five years.

The Four Seasons Calendar. Each calendar is made up of four paintings, one for each season of the year. In most of the calendars (I've done one every year since 1947) I used the same characters in all four paintings; each painting showed them engaged in an activity appropriate to the season which it represented: four boys playing basketball, baseball, golf, and football (below right). In several calendars the link between the four paintings has been thematic: The Four Ages of Love (above, Spring, or young love).

COURTESY BROWN AND BIGELOW

A mural painted for the Nassau Tavern in Princeton, New Jersey. The costumes are authentic; the incident is apocryphal. I did research on the uniforms of the Hessian and British soldiers who fought around Princeton during the Revolution and had copies of them made by a costumer. But Yankee Doodle is a mythical character. The

COURTESY THE BERKSHIRE LIFE INSURANCE COMPANY

A balloon ascension in Pittsfield, Massachusetts, circa 1854: the color sketch of a mural for the Berkshire Life Insurance Company, which was founded in Pittsfield in 1854.

lyrics of the song do not state what town he "came to" (or "went to"; there are several versions, and no one seems to be able to decide which is the original), and, to top it all off, the lyrics are said to have been written in 1755, twenty years before the Revolution.

The color sketch of "Dover Coach," an illustration. The original painting now hangs over the bar in the clubhouse of the Society of Illustrators in New York.

"Treasures." One of many attic pictures I painted at one period, principally because a window in my studio gave the same lighting effect as an attic window.

"The New Tavern Sign." Like a *Post* cover, the subject picture, of which all the paintings on these two pages are examples, tells a story.

"Hollywood Dreams."

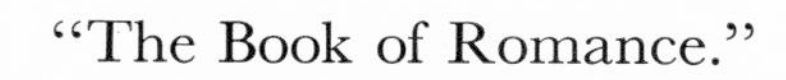

"The Book of Romance."

But unlike a *Post* cover, it is titled and has a caption. It is usually a quieter picture, lacking the immediate impact of a *Post* cover.

"The Silhouette."

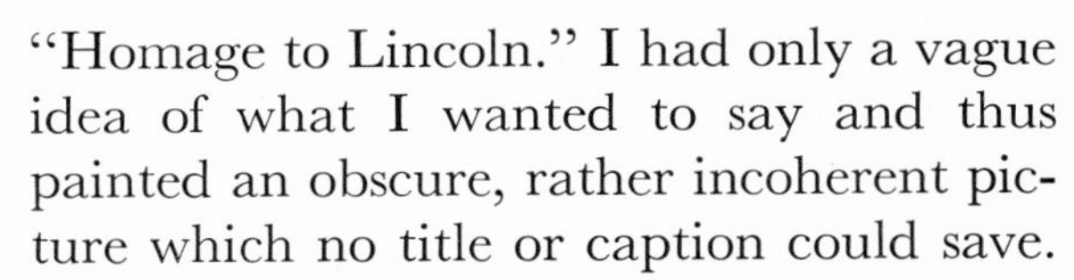

"Homage to Lincoln." I had only a vague idea of what I wanted to say and thus painted an obscure, rather incoherent picture which no title or caption could save.

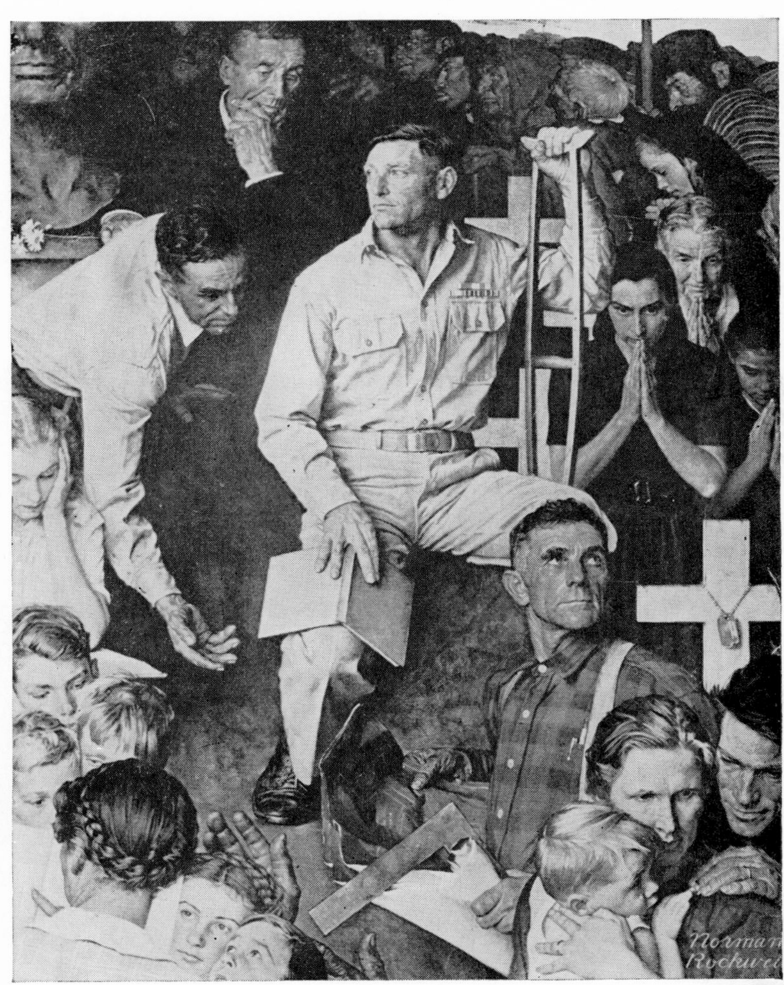

"Christmas Reunion."

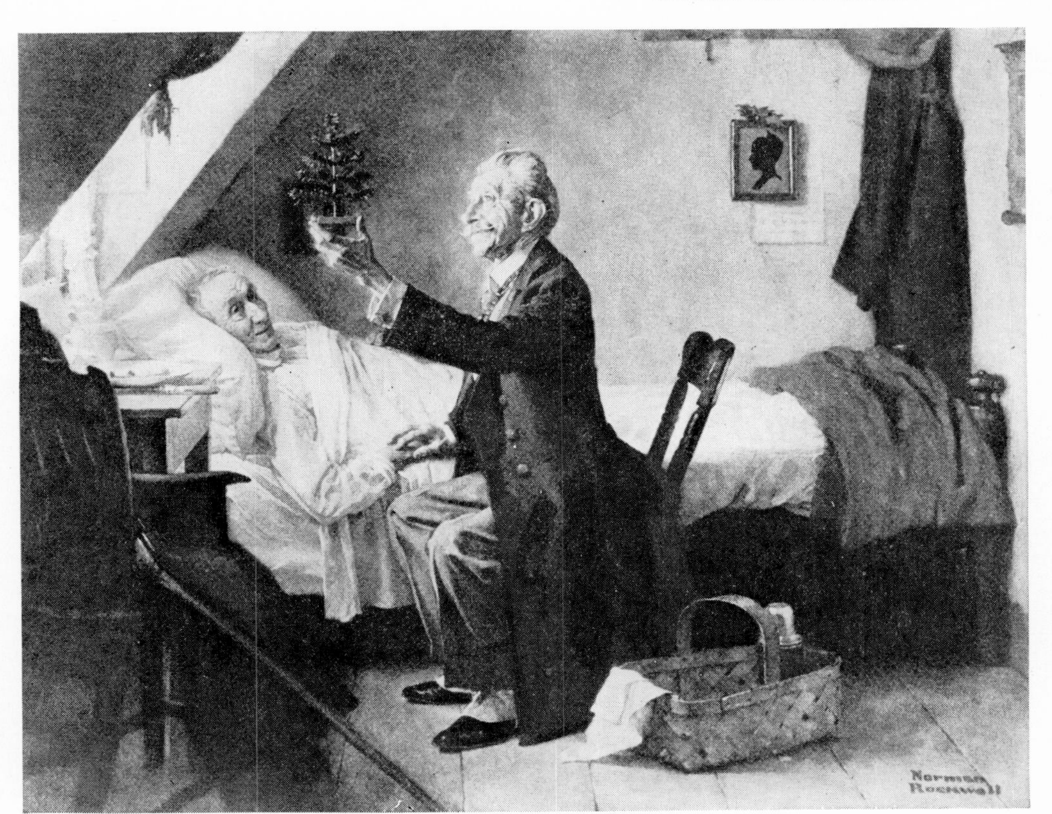

A watercolor of Henry Ford driving through Detroit in his first automobile. Painted for the fiftieth-anniversary calendar of the Ford Motor Company.

One of a series of ads I did for Fisk tires during the early 1920s. All were based on the slogan "Time to Re-Tire" and depicted various picturesque characters fast asleep. The soft sell.

The only battle picture I've ever done other than a few very early illustrations for young people's magazines. I don't like to do pictures which glorify killing, even in a good cause.

One of a series of ads. Note the pun: socks by Interwoven, "socks" on the boy's rump. I don't remember whether it was my pun or the advertising agency's.

Two ads from a recent campaign I've been doing for the Massachusetts Mutual Life Insurance Company. The puzzled voter is me.

An ad for Edison Mazda Lamp Works.

An ad for The Watchmakers of Switzerland. One of my best, I think, though it was painted in a small hotel room by artificial light.

Jennifer Jones in the movie *The Song of Bernadette*.

I don't particularly like to do posters; they're sheer propaganda; all the people in them have to be handsome, honest, healthy, strong.

COURTESY HALLMARK CARDS

Christmas cards. I select traditional subjects—Santa Claus, kids, Christmas revelers, or a cup of Christmas cheer in merry old England—for the cards I do, because that's the way I feel about Christmas. I don't like cards which try to be sophisticated, ultramodern, or cynically clever.

For some years now I have wanted to do a series of pictures which could be published as a book. I have toyed with many ideas for such a series, but nothing ever came of any of them, though I did start work on a couple. I painted a picture of Johnny Appleseed for a proposed series of characters from American folklore, and did charcoal preliminaries of Horatio Alger's Phil the Fiddler (right) and Frances Hodgson Burnett's Little Lord Fauntleroy (below left) for a series of celebrated characters from American juvenile classics. I don't remember why I gave up these series; they might have made rather nice books. Perhaps I'll take them up again sometime.

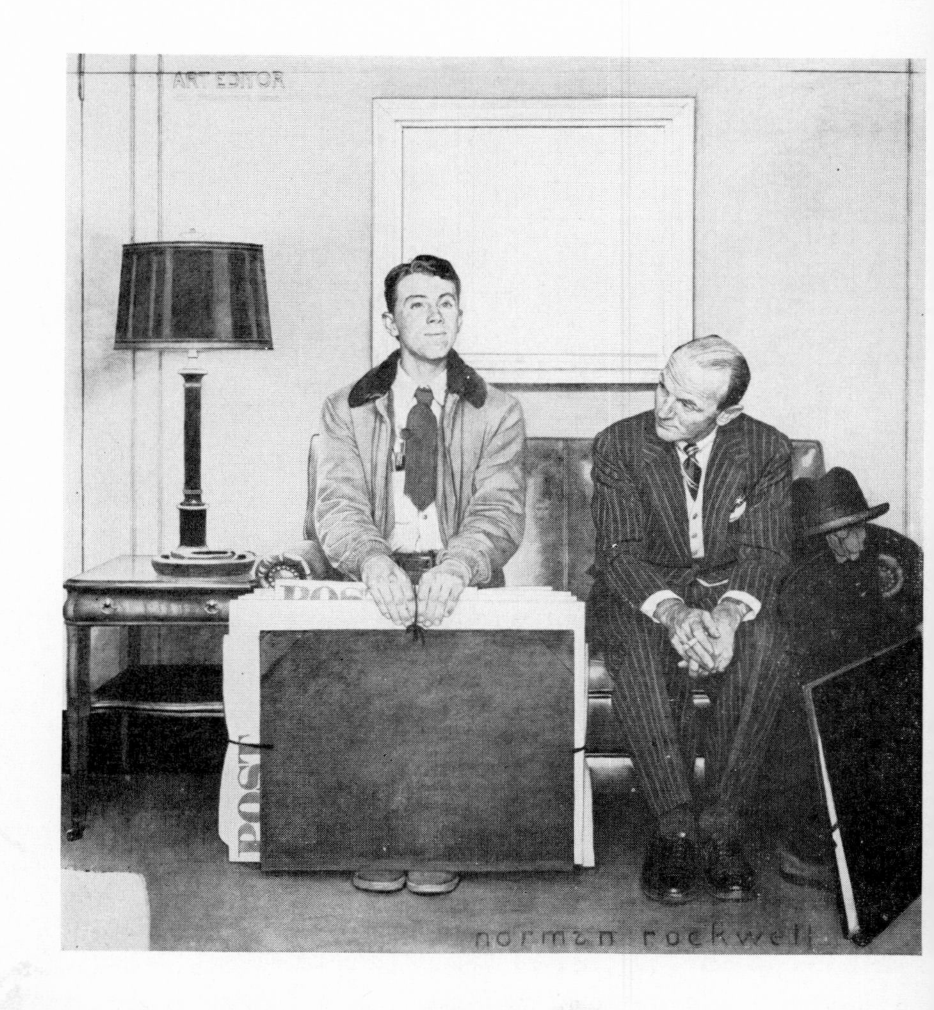

The charcoal drawing of a *Post* cover idea—the hopeful young illustrator and the worldly-wise professional seated outside the art editor's office—which was discarded when the idea proved too tenuous and vague.

This charcoal drawing of a street scene in Karachi, Pakistan, was developed from a sketch done during my trip around the world in 1958. I submitted it to Pan American Airways as a proposed ad, but it was rejected, so I did not make a painting of it.

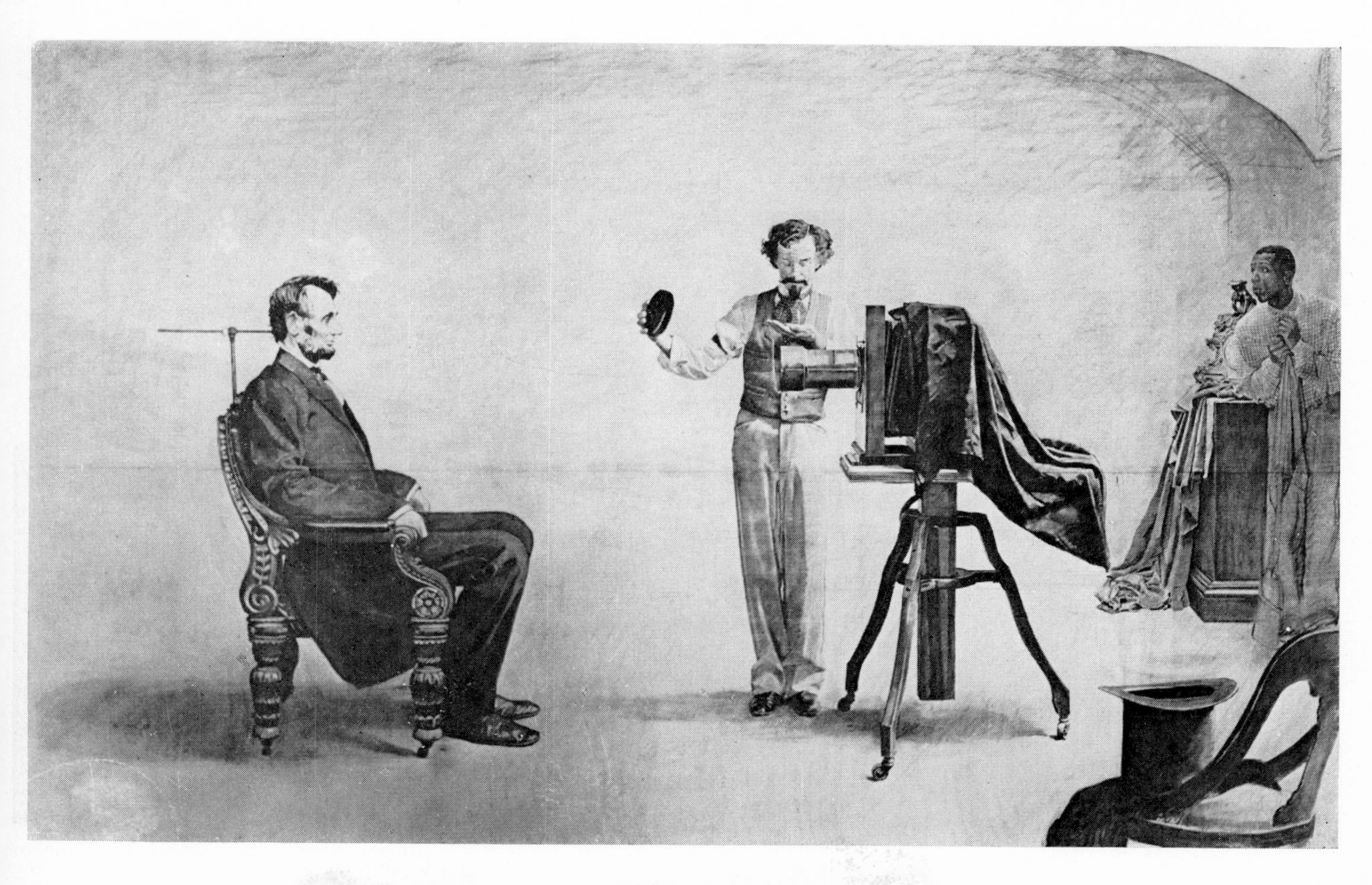

I have always been fascinated by Lincoln and over the years have attempted a number of paintings of him. Some years ago I completed one of him delivering the Gettysburg Address, but since then, for one reason or another, I have failed to finish any of the paintings of him which I started. This charcoal drawing of Matthew Brady photographing Lincoln is an example.

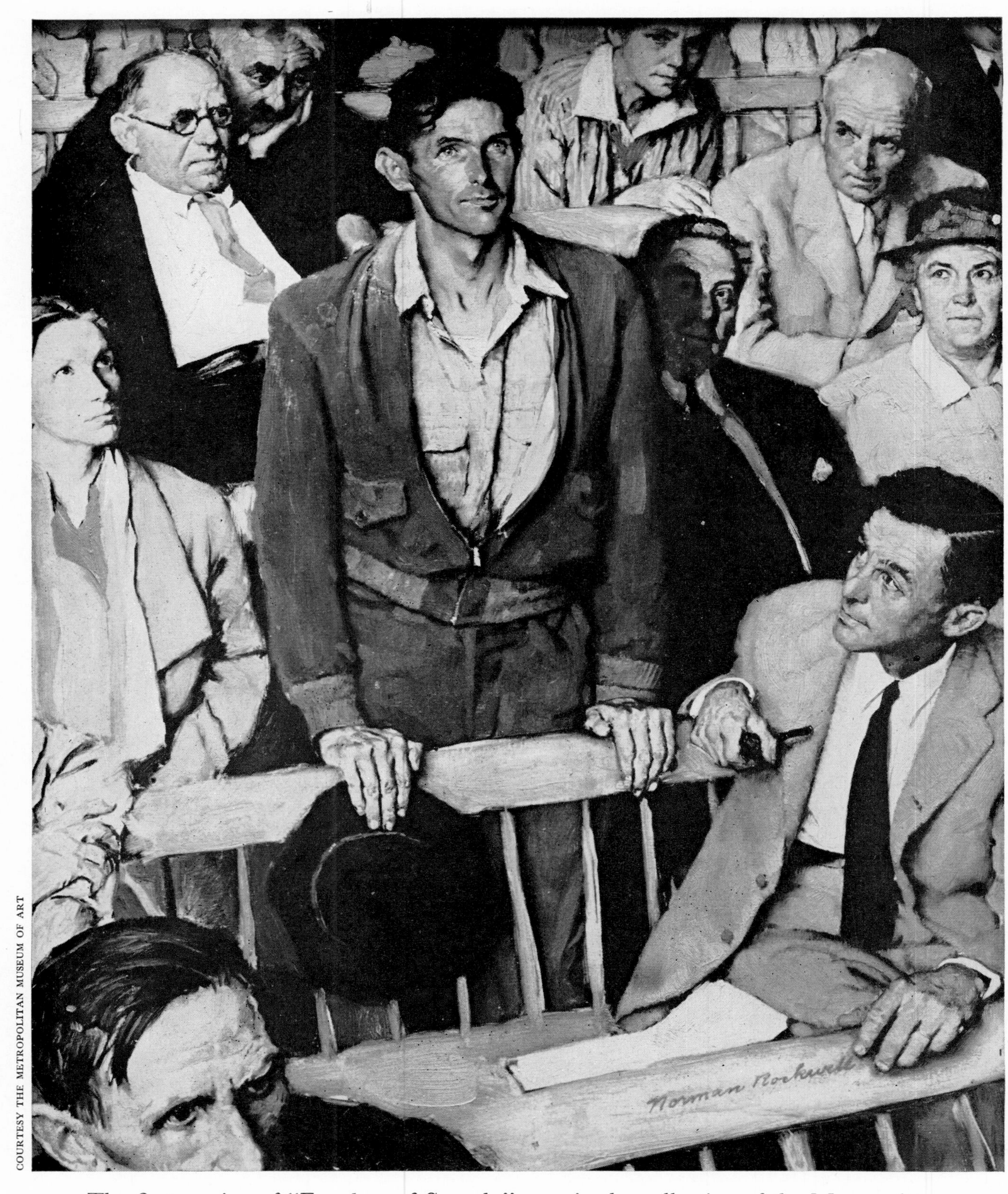

The first version of "Freedom of Speech," now in the collection of the Metropolitan Museum of Art.

THE FOUR FREEDOMS

In the future days, which we seek to make secure, we look forward to a world founded upon four essential human freedoms.

The first is freedom of speech and expression—everywhere in the world.

The second is freedom of every person to worship God in his own way—everywhere in the world.

The third is freedom from want—which, translated into world terms, means economic understandings which will secure to every nation a healthy peacetime life for its inhabitants—everywhere in the world.

The fourth is freedom from fear—which, translated into world terms, means a world-wide reduction of armaments to such a point and in such a thorough fashion that no nation will be in a position to commit an act of physical aggression against any neighbor—anywhere in the world.

FRANKLIN DELANO ROOSEVELT
in the Annual Message to the Congress
January 6, 1941

FREEDOM OF SPEECH

NORMAN ROCKWEL
L REPORT

FREEDOM OF WORSHIP

EACH ACCORDING TO THE DICTATES
OF HIS OWN CONSCIENCE
NORMAN ROCKWELL

FREEDOM FROM WANT

Norman
Rockwell

FREEDOM FROM FEAR

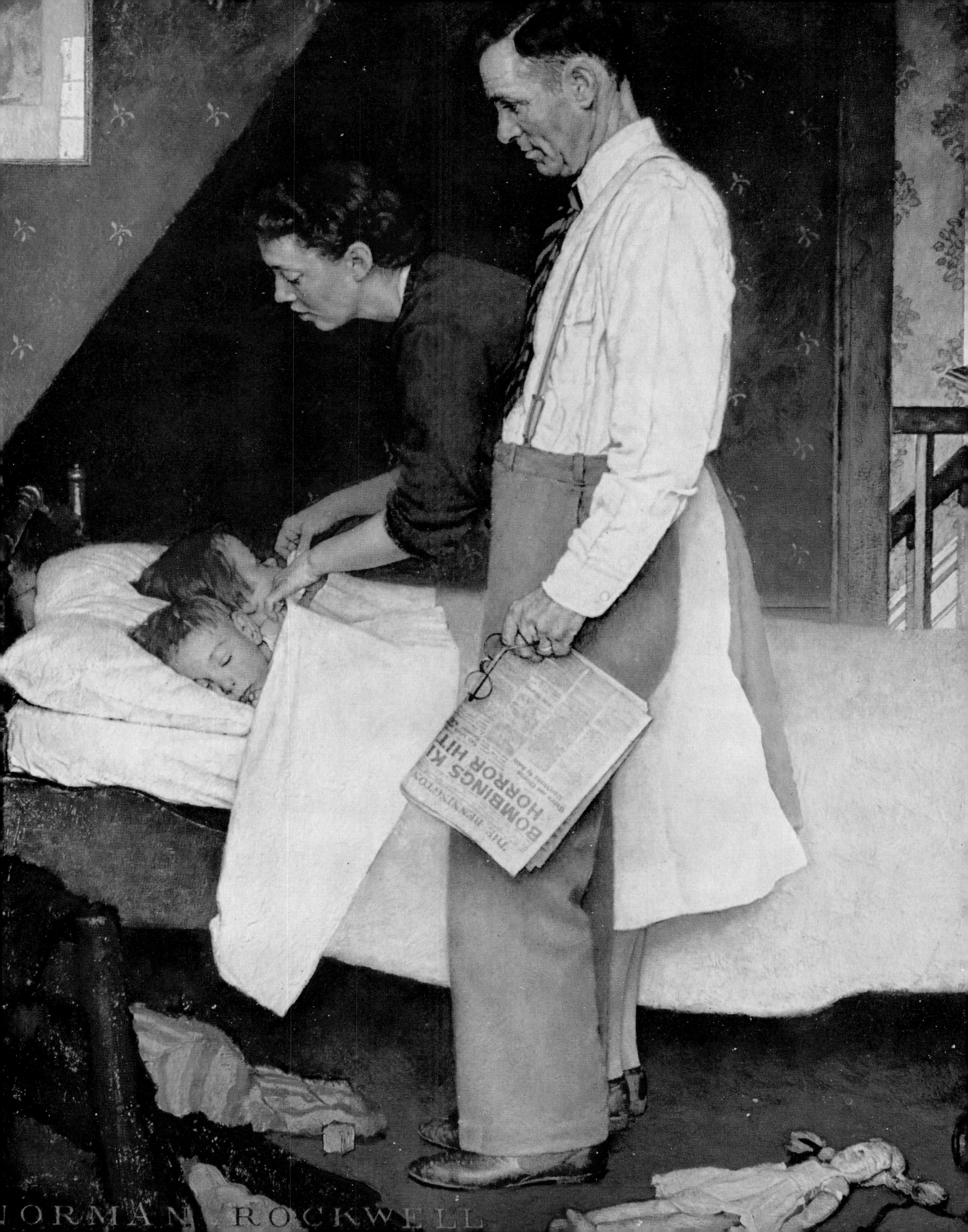
BOMBINGS
HORROR
ROCKWELL

A MATTER OF OPINION

It is naturally difficult to take seriously an artist who provides as much fun as Norman Rockwell does, and he is not often taken seriously by the people who live in the world of fine arts. I think this is a mistake. Each generation produces definitions of art and theories of aesthetics, but in perspective they tend to reflect the taste of the generation more than anything else. There are certain facts about Mr. Rockwell which make me feel he deserves long and serious consideration, between the periods of pure entertainment which he produces so prolifically. He is qualified because he knows the craft of putting life in the round on a flat surface. His work evokes a response which in terms of people is probably greater than that of any artist who ever lived. This vast audience responds naturally, without art-appreciation classes, and it appears to include a full range of intellectual, environmental, and age levels. This appreciation has spanned almost a half century, during which time great changes in taste have taken place. These facts do not spell beauty—but they do describe a kind of universality that may very well be essential to art.

The controversy about Mr. Rockwell's relative merits as a fine artist appears to originate in his choice of subject matter and in his approach to it. The former has been declared trivial and unrealistic, the latter, mechanical and too realistic. The necessity of selecting profound subjects in order to qualify pictures for acceptance as works of art has been proved untrue so often that the reverse of this premise is virtually a cornerstone of contemporary aesthetics. Criticism centering around Norman Rockwell's photographic style is natural in a time when subjectless expression is most appreciated.

What is Mr. Rockwell painting about? He has painted so much that it is difficult to generalize. He always portrays people, and usually at an instant in time when some emotional or atmospheric quality is at its height. The point of these pictures is to communicate the emotion to the viewer so that he can either experience it himself or react to it as an outsider. For example, one shares the keen embarrassment of the boy on the 1916 *Post* cover who wheels his baby sister past his friends on their way to play baseball. The props are so familiar to a certain generation of viewers that self-identification is immediate, but the phenomena involved—forced separation of the individual from the group and the assignation of the function of one sex to the other—are basic human situations which involve all of us vicariously, regardless of age and environment. The 1920 cover of the departing maid sweeping by the armorial bearings of her trade evokes first amusement and then a sense of sympathy for the characteristically human vanity which makes her extend her little finger so daintily. Christmas of 1934 the *Post* gave us Norman Rockwell's Tiny Tim on the shoulders of Bob Cratchit, with those famous words that carry so much joy because of their proximity to tragedy. The portrayal of these two characters of Dickens makes of the words a profound and unforgettable image that does not require a knowledge of *The Christmas Carol* or of nineteenth-century England. There are so many others which grab our attention at first glance and then continue to delight us as recognition of the subject grows.

The departing maid.

This immediacy of communication appears to be one of the reasons why the creator of these images is not universally accepted as a fine artist. We have become so used to searching for meaning in human creation that to consider the obvious seems superficial. I think that there are two reasons for the lack of appreciation of Mr. Rockwell's work among patrons of the arts. The first is that we have a colossal cultural guilt complex, born of the number of artists—such as van Gogh and Ryder—whose genius was not recognized during their lifetime. This complex has filled us with a dread of making similar mistakes and a determination to recognize quality wherever we think it appears. Men like

Tiny Tim and Bob Cratchit.

Mr. Rockwell, who are commercially successful and very famous, do not come within this complex simply because they are already "doing all right." The second reason is that Mr. Rockwell is not known by his original work but by its mechanical interpretation via color reproduction. This is particularly unfortunate in view of the "too photographic" criticism. The spontaneity with which the tools of his trade are handled is not easily visible in reproduction, and this element is essential to the proper evaluation of his "expression."

When this last half century is explored by the future, a few paintings will continue to communicate with the same immediacy and veracity that they have today. I believe that some of Mr. Rockwell's will be among them.

THOMAS S. BUECHNER
Director, The Brooklyn Museum

RECENT *POST* COVERS

NR painting NR, by NR.

This would have been a better cover if I had not caricatured the people. I noticed my mistake while painting the first version (above), and started the picture over. But though I toned down the caricature, I did not eliminate it entirely. I often caricature when I shouldn't. I fail to see the people as real people, I oversimplify, try to make them too cute—in this instance, a cute little family. I don't do it satirically, to poke fun at the people. . . . I added the roofs and church steeple to the background in the final version because I thought the steeple with its clanging bell (I tried to indicate the sound by painting in the birds flying up from the steeple) clarified the story which I wanted to tell. Without it, one might not have realized that the family is going to church. With it, one is certain of their destination and even, to a certain extent, of their route: up the block and around the corner.

SILVER SLIPPER
GRILL
ROOMS
norman rockwell

A black eye isn't black. It's a hash of colors—blue, purple, a little green, a touch of yellow, crimson, orange, magenta. Nor is it just a simple swelling. It's a complicated puffiness. But I didn't know that when I set out to paint this little girl's black eye. I figured it would be easy. But then I tried to paint it and found I couldn't get it right, no matter how hard I worked. I decided I'd have to find a kid with a genuine black eye and paint it from life. I called our local doctors. No, they didn't know of any black eyes in town. I called the school. No. Hospital? No. There wasn't a black eye in all of Bennington County. The next day I had to go to Pittsfield, Massachusetts. I stopped in at the hospital there. Sorry, no black eyes. Dr. Robert W. Gladstone, the anesthetist, referred me to his brother-in-law, Sidney R. Kanter, a photographer. He might know of a black eye among his many customers. He didn't, but suggested that we ask the local newspaper, the *Berkshire Eagle*, to run a story describing my problem. The editors agreed. I said I'd pay $5.00 to the bearer of a ripe black eye. Several people responded but none had the eye I was looking for. Then the wire services picked up the story. And all of a sudden I was deluged with black eyes. A father of five children wrote that for $5.00 he'd *give* all five of his children black eyes and I could take my pick. The warden of a prison down South wrote that there had been a riot in his prison and he had *four hundred* black eyes available. I received letters from as far away as England. Then a grandfather in Springfield, Massachusetts, sent me a detailed description of his grandson's black eye and offered to drive the boy up to my studio in Arlington. I accepted his offer, it was a beauty, I made a color sketch, and the cover was finished.

PRINCI
Norman
Rockwell

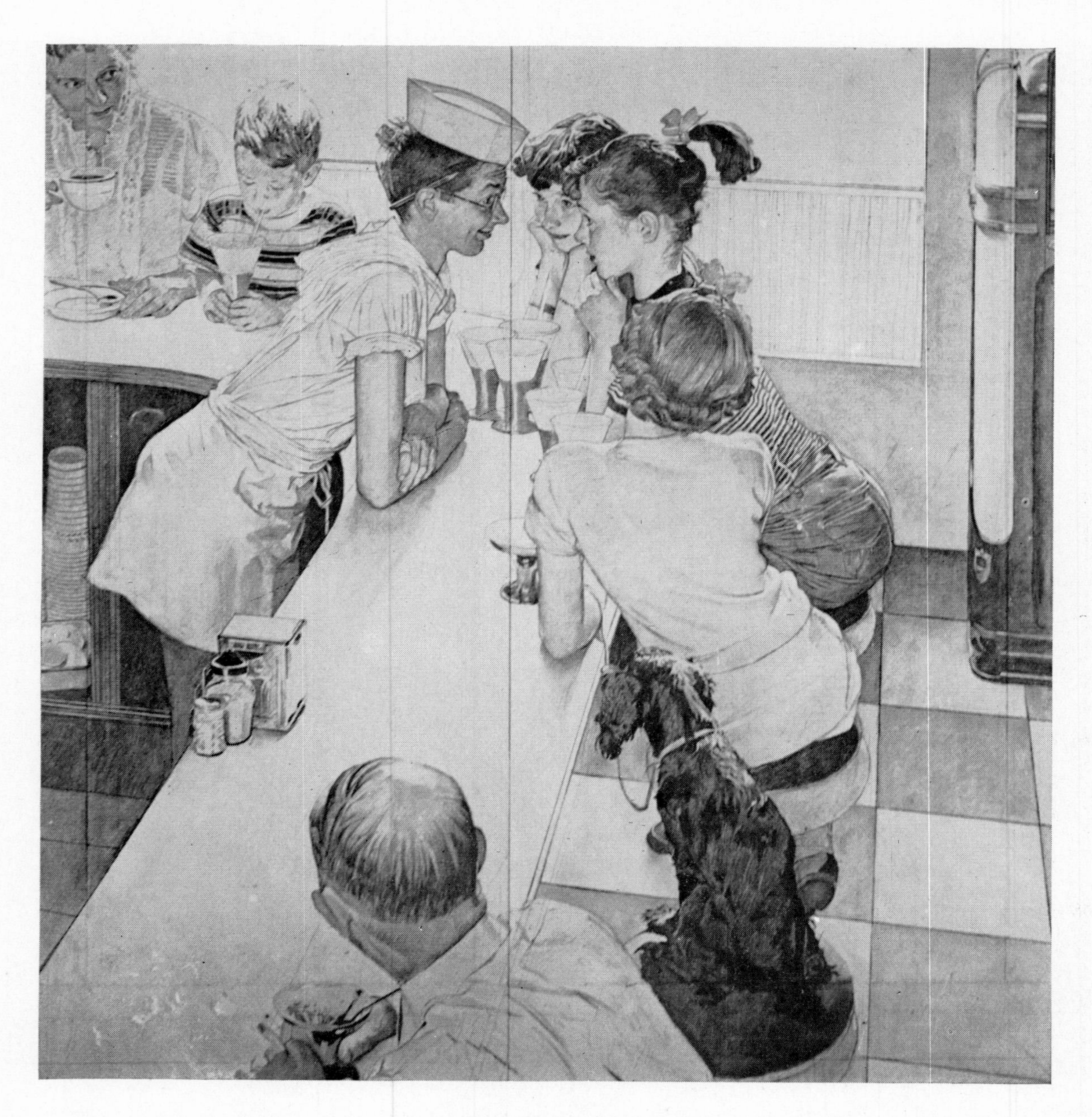

I painted this cover twice. After I had finished the first version (above), I decided that the man in the foreground and the lady and boy in the upper left corner were unnecessary distractions, confusing the cover. I wanted to depict a youthful soda jerk who is popular with the girls because he is in a position to dispense favors—an extra-large scoop of ice cream, a generous ooze of hot fudge. I thought I'd better concentrate on the soda jerk. So in the final version I eliminated the three superfluous people and added the jealous young dude to point up the unique and enviable position enjoyed by the soda jerk. In painting the second version I greatly reduced the size of the painting. Serious subjects seem to demand a large canvas; light or humorous subjects, a small one. . . . I got the idea for the cover from my youngest son Peter's accounts of his experiences while working in a soda fountain the previous summer. He posed for the central figure, but was not particularly pleased with the portrait: "I'm not that goofy-looking," he said.

Norman
Rockwell

My original sketch of the idea.

The king of beasts eyes the slab of horse-meat warily. He has just tried and failed to claw it into his cage.

An example of the purely humorous cover; a burlesque; low comedy. It is a joke, nothing more, provoking only a laugh. At the sight and smell of the keeper's overflowing sandwich (I always thought that bit of meat dangling from the sandwich was a good touch), the proud king of beasts becomes just a sad and hungry cat. I usually try to make a cover mean something more than just a gag. Not that I don't enjoy painting this kind of cover. It's easier: I sort of breeze along, chuckling (immodestly) to myself.

The king of beasts nobly contemplates his own digestive processes, having just eaten the horsemeat. These photographs were taken at the Bronx Zoo in New York City.

GUARD
Norman
Rockwell

GENE PELHAM, PHOTOGRAPHER

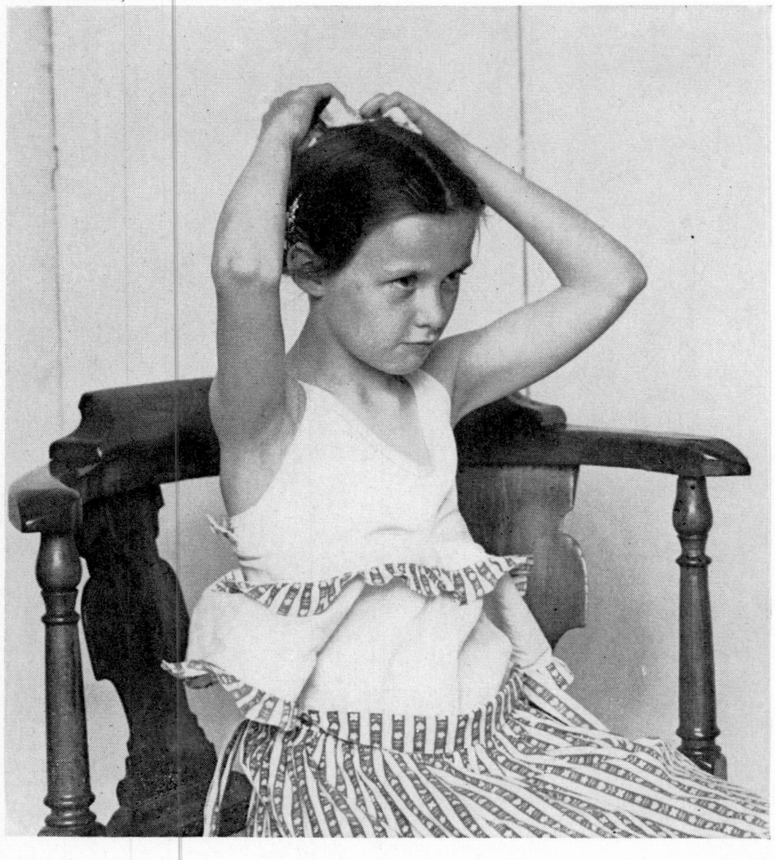

The model, Mary Whalen, primping. I am sorry to say that she has since grown up. She was the best little-girl model I ever had. She could assume any expression I requested: sad, merry, joyful, wistful, disdainful. Her body was as expressive as her face.

The first rough sketch of the idea. As a kid, I used to contemplate myself in a mirror, wondering if I was handsome.

The final sketch of the idea. I should not have added the photograph of the movie star. The little girl is not wondering if she looks like the star, but just trying to estimate her own charms.

ORMAN ROCKWELL

On Sundays in the choir room we roughhoused and shouted and wrestled while donning our cassocks and surplices. The sexton, poking his head around the door, would yell that it was time for us to enter the church. Plastering down our cowlicks, pushing, jostling, we'd form two lines. Then, suddenly, we'd grow quiet and, solemn-faced, march into the church. The first sketch of this cover (above), inspired by these memories, has more spirit and liveliness than the finished painting. But then I began to fool with it and slightly obscured the original, simple statement. The painting is a bit too cluttered and busy, the archway too close in tone to the scene it frames. I began by trying to improve on the sketch and ended by losing some of its vitality and freshness. I should have put more trust in my original inspiration. Of course, I am rarely satisfied with a painting.

First version.

Second version.

In theme at least, this cover is autobiographical. I was trying to express what a father feels when his son leaves home. Jerry, my oldest son, had enlisted in the Air Force; my younger sons, Tom and Peter, had gone away to school. Whenever I feel an idea strongly, I have trouble painting it. I keep trying to refine it, express it better. With the exception of the sketch (right), the pictures on this page are charcoal preliminaries. As you can see, I could not decide on the proper setting. None seemed to convey the idea that the boy was leaving home to go to college. By the time I had discarded the third charcoal, I had begun to lose confidence in my original conception. I decided to add the mother. A rough sketch showed me that her presence added nothing. After trying the station platform, I returned to the original setting, substituting the trunk and signal lamp for the mailbag, the rail for the edge of the platform.

Fourth version.

Third version.

Fifth version.

RANCH
STATE U.
Norman
Rockwell

"Anyone who remains calm in the midst of all this confusion simply does not understand the situation."—BENJAMIN FRANKLIN

SCOVILL, PHOTOGRAPHER

The original sketch.

Whenever someone comes into my studio, I ask his opinion of the picture I'm working on. I evaluate his suggestions, perhaps adopting one or two, perhaps rejecting all. But sometimes I'm so befuddled that I cannot sort out all the suggestions. The picture is going badly; I'm doubting myself. I adopt all suggestions desperately. That was the case with this cover. I could not determine what the woman in the portrait should look like, what her expression should be. And everyone who came into the studio and gave his opinion had a different opinion. I don't remember how many sketches I made of the woman; at least twenty. Nor do I remember how I finally arrived at a decision. Perhaps one day I locked the door; maybe one day two visitors gave the same advice. I had other troubles with the painting. In the photograph above you can see the first version (partially obscured by the palette table). A harrowing experience.

I begin with a rather foolish Dutch *Hausfrau*, more puzzled than angry, her nose awry.

Someone asks, "Don't you think she should be more cowlike? You know, placid, accepting?"

Someone states (categorically), "She should be furiously indignant with that snooping young upstart."

Someone suggests, "Do you think she should be a peasant? How about an indignant duchess?"

Someone moans, "Oh, *no-o-o*. A duchess wouldn't deign to notice a sneakered art student."

Someone laughs, "But she would enjoy it! After two hundred years in a frame! Maybe a little piqued too."

I'm going nuts. "Calm her down." "Don't caricature." "Make her more bosomy." "A nicer person."

I'm tired; so are my advisors. "I don't know. Try an arch, amused look. You've got me."

norman rockwell

The most important difference between the first sketch (above) and the finished painting is in the pose of the license clerk. In the sketch he is watching the young couple; in the painting he is gazing dreamily at nothing, half bored, half sad; romance is routine to him. This change in his pose occurred as the result of a happy accident. Jason Braman, a beloved citizen of Stockbridge, was the model for the clerk. He, the young couple (who were actually engaged at the time and married soon after), my photographer, and I were in the Stockbridge town offices. While I posed the young couple, Mr. Braman sat in the chair behind the desk, waiting until I got around to him. I happened to glance at him. He was sitting just as I have painted him, with the same expression on his face. I realized immediately that it was a far better pose than the one I had sketched. That proved to be the key to the cover. The other changes—adding the cat and the potbellied stove, omitting the second couple entering the office—were incidental.

MARRIAGE LICENSES
HOUSATONIC
SATURDAY
11
JUNE
norman rockwell

The mermaid seems to have been slightly controversial. Letters received by the *Post* and printed in the Letters to the Editors department in the issues of 24 September and 22 October, 1955:

Dear Sirs:
. . . My whole family as well as thousands of people have always regarded the *Post* as a reputable magazine, one which we would not hesitate to display on our magazine racks, but you have reduced it to one which any decent American would rather be without or hide, because of the obscene picture on the cover. . . .

SUSANNE LACHAPELLE
Worcester, Mass.

Dear Sirs:
. . . My native caution prompts me to ask for expert advice. . . .

What bait is best? Where are the best fishin' holes (or grounds)? What about a license? Do they keep well, or spoil readily? And what about fishing regulations (limit, etc.)?

ALVIN MAHNKE
Three Rivers, Mich.

Dear Sirs:
. . . I note by your *Post* of Sept. 24 that the sensibilities of a subscriber in Massachusetts were disturbed because of your [Norman Rockwell] cover, August 20. . . . Our sensibilities were not disturbed, but had the lobsterman dropped the mermaid in a pot of boiling water, we would have been enraged!!! . . .

DR. E. A. E. PALMQUIST, *Minister*
Woodland Baptist Church
Philadelphia, Pa.

Dear Sirs:
. . . About the mermaid: Some people don't have a funny bone left in their bodies. . . .

MRS. MARGARET BIERSCHENK
Pennsauken, N. J.

Dear Sirs:
. . . Do not like lobsters, but think mermaids O. K. . . .

JOSEPH L. CHAPMAN
Margate City, N. J.

Dear Sirs:
. . . Your mermaid cover is delightful. I would love my husband to catch one if only he also would go and trap a faun for me. . . .

MRS. VICKY SMITS
Sudbury, Canada

Dear Sirs:
Norman Rockwell couldn't draw an obscene picture!! . . .

MRS. JAMES E. GASTON
Fairhope, Ala.

Dear Sirs:
. . . What could be cleaner than a young innocent mermaid fresh drawn from the water? . . .

L. W. DAVIS
Meshoppen, Pa.

Dear Sirs:
. . . What did you expect a mermaid to wear? A sweatshirt? . . .

MRS. M. H. WILLIAMS
Tangent, Oregon

Dear Sirs:
Norman Rockwell's mermaid cover obscene? Aw fiddle!!

AGNES REESE
Westminster, Md.

Dear Sirs:
. . . Now that this cover has appeared, I'm not only wondering about the artist (whom I've always considered wonderful), but I'm also wondering about the editors (you) who would let such a cover be published. . . .

PEG NEWMAN
Schenectady, N. Y.

*The vote on Rockwell's cover at press time was: In Poor Taste, 11; Obscene, 21; Not Obscene, 245.—Editor's Note.

W.E.M. LOBSTERS
LOBSTERS
norman rockwell

I painted this cover as a sort of tribute to schoolteachers—in particular, my favorite teacher, Miss Julia Smith, who taught me all the history, arithmetic, grammar, and geography I know and encouraged me to draw: at Christmastime, Santa Claus and his reindeer in colored chalks on the blackboard; in geography class, Arabs and Indians; in history, covered wagons and Puritans. . . . I made the sketch (right) while painting the cover, because I had lost track of what I wanted to express in the portrait of the schoolteacher—the selfless devotion of teachers, willing to work long hours for their students. A quick sketch sometimes helps me to regain the freshness and vitality of my original inspiration.

Happy Birthday
Miss Jones
Suprise
Birthday
happy
Surprise
surprise
Teacher
Surprise
Jones
Birthday Jonesy
Jones
norman rockwell

An unpopular cover. People don't enjoy pictures of a child's disillusionment with Christmas. I thought we could get around this by publishing the cover in August. But the editors decided to publish it in December. Of course, it's not much of a cover, anyway. . . . I got kind of gay with the beard. I'd tacked a false beard on my easel and was trying to paint it so that every hair would look real. But a beard is awful hairy, and after a while I got tired. So I pulled some hair out of the beard and stuck it in the wet paint on the canvas. Visitors to the studio said, "Gee, that beard is realistically painted." This sort of thing is not art, and I know it, but it's fun.

norman rockwell

I call this my chinless picture. If you'll notice, not one of the characters in it possesses a normal chin—all weak as polliwogs. I even concealed the chin of the man on the left behind his shoulder. I don't know why. How much more delightful the cover would have been if I had painted the models as they really were—a sweet, pretty girl, a good-looking boy. I had intended to paint a warm, pleasant picture—a young girl after her first prom. But then I was overcome by an irresistible impulse to caricature. Enough said. I sometimes think I'll never learn.

Real ITALIAN
HAM
Norman Rockwell

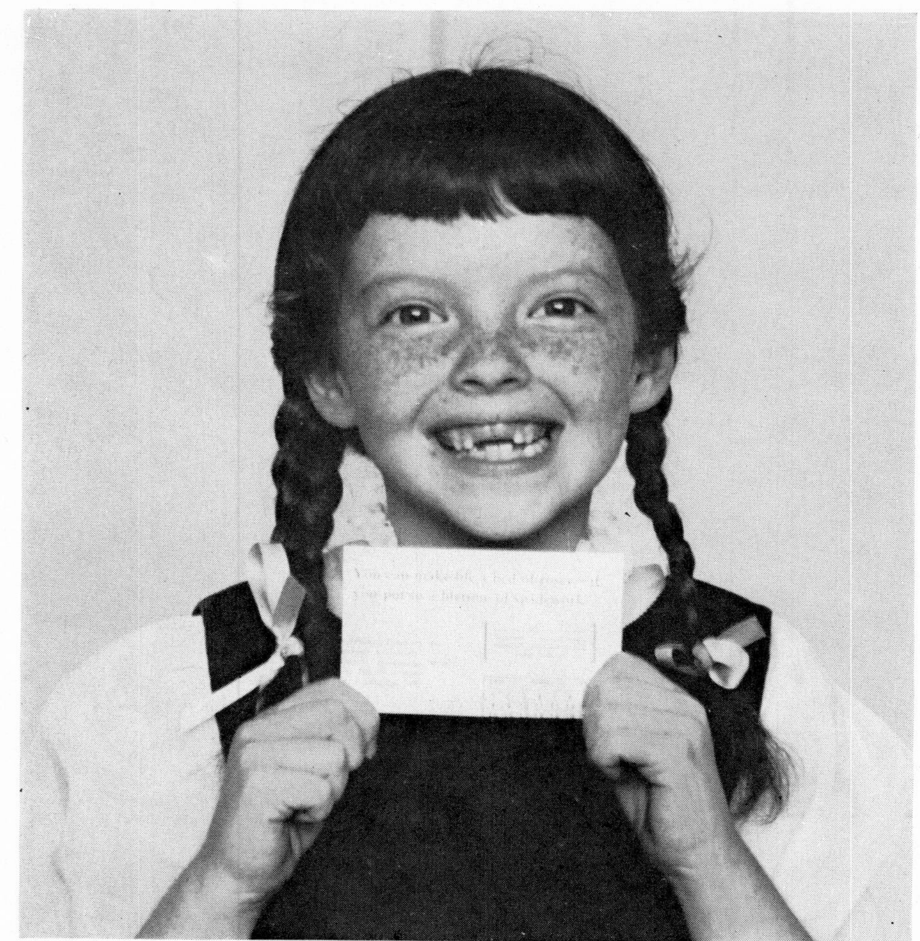

SCOVILL, PHOTOGRAPHER

Anne Morgan posing for the ad.

I was painting a series of advertisements for Crest toothpaste: "Look, Mom—no cavities!" I asked Anne Morgan, the daughter of friends, to pose for one of the ads. When she showed up at the studio, she had two front teeth missing. It was a simple matter to paint in the teeth for the ad, but it set me to thinking. This *Post* cover was the result. I did not use Anne as a model for the cover; I didn't think it would be fair to Crest. The model I did use had no missing teeth. So I had to paint *out* her teeth.

The advertisement for Crest toothpaste.

Norman
Rockwell

[illegible]

Think whole figure and accessories should be painted in strong down light. it will give the late at night, "desperate" quality. Maybe paint it in cold almost bluish light. My "blue period" expense acct.

[illegible]
LUNCHES #63.00
DINNERS #85.00
ENTETAIN MENT x this is where he's stuck

Pullman towel

gadget for adjusting chair back

railway tickets

Theatre stubs

I don't know drawing of Pullman chair Think when it is correct it will be recognizable

Stork Club and "21" etc folders

boxes of cigars to be smoked at home

Dear Ken —
I think this, along with you wonderful idea of the entire
is swell. "Glad Hand Charlie" has his
expense acct. background, I believe with an authentic Pullman chair it will
problem. place him without the mix up than I've indicated with the tissue.
any and all suggestions most welcome Yours Norman

The rough sketch which I submitted to Ken Stuart, Art Editor of the *Post*.

From M. to M. Total days

See other side of sheet for instructions

EXPENSE ACCOUNT

Name Ernest Hall DATE Nov. 22, 1957

Items D 11-18 11-19 11-2 11-22

Approved

Rail and A 50.79 5.08

Sleeping a 1.25 1.25

Name of Ho The St. R

Hotel Expen 16.80

Charge Account

Breakfast

Lunch

Dinner -411-68

Total Amount

Street Cars, Taxi, B

Tel. and Tel.

Entertaining

Baggage ,60

Signed

Total

Date Amount

.57 *Dinner and en bridge

C. Segar, Eu 70

.57 Entertainment, 65

.57 Dinner — Mr. + M 18 40

.1.57 *Luncheon and enter T. McCarthy

Miss Charlotte Cavanaugh $16 35

21.57 Dinner · Frank Sellars, Francis Brennan, E. Schneider

Entertainment — H. Neelen

Norman Rockwell

The first sketch.

I guess everyone has sat at one time or another in a doctor's office and examined his diplomas, wondering how good a doctor he was. . . . This cover occasioned a great argument among my family and friends: how much of the boy's fanny should be showing. Some said more, some less. I finally locked the door of the studio and, after communing with myself for some time, lowered his pants to their present position, a compromise which avoids shocking nudity and yet reveals enough to provoke humor.

PHOTOGRAPHS BY CLEMENS KALISCHER

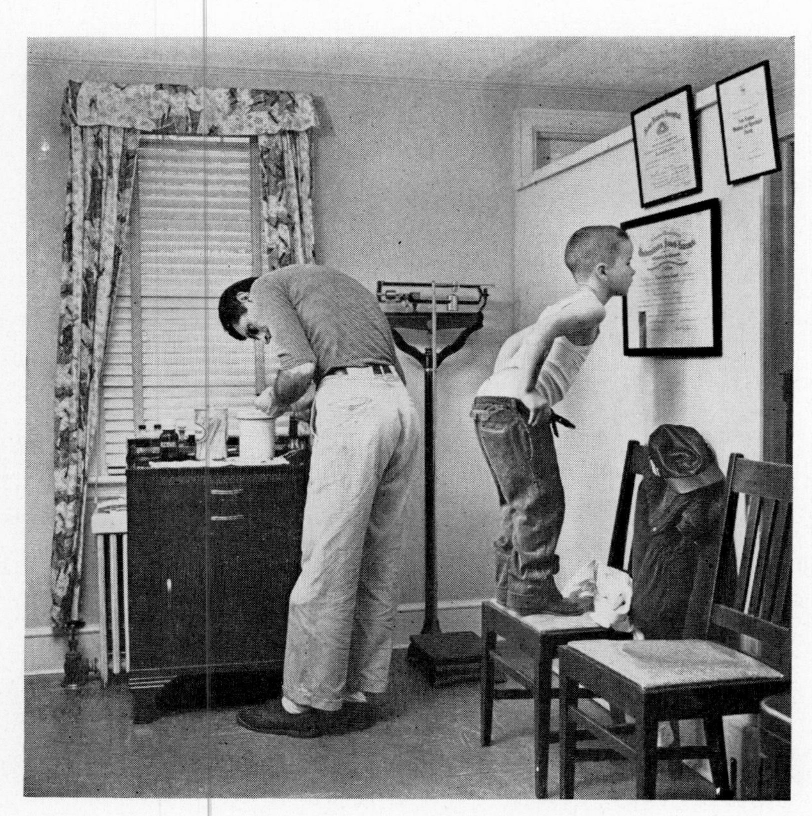

The interior of Dr. Donald Campbell's office here in Stockbridge. Dr. Campbell was the model for the doctor, but while the little boy posed, Louis Lamone, my man Friday, acted as the doctor's stand-in.

Terry Locke, the model for the little boy, stuffs his shirt into his pants and watches me write out his check.

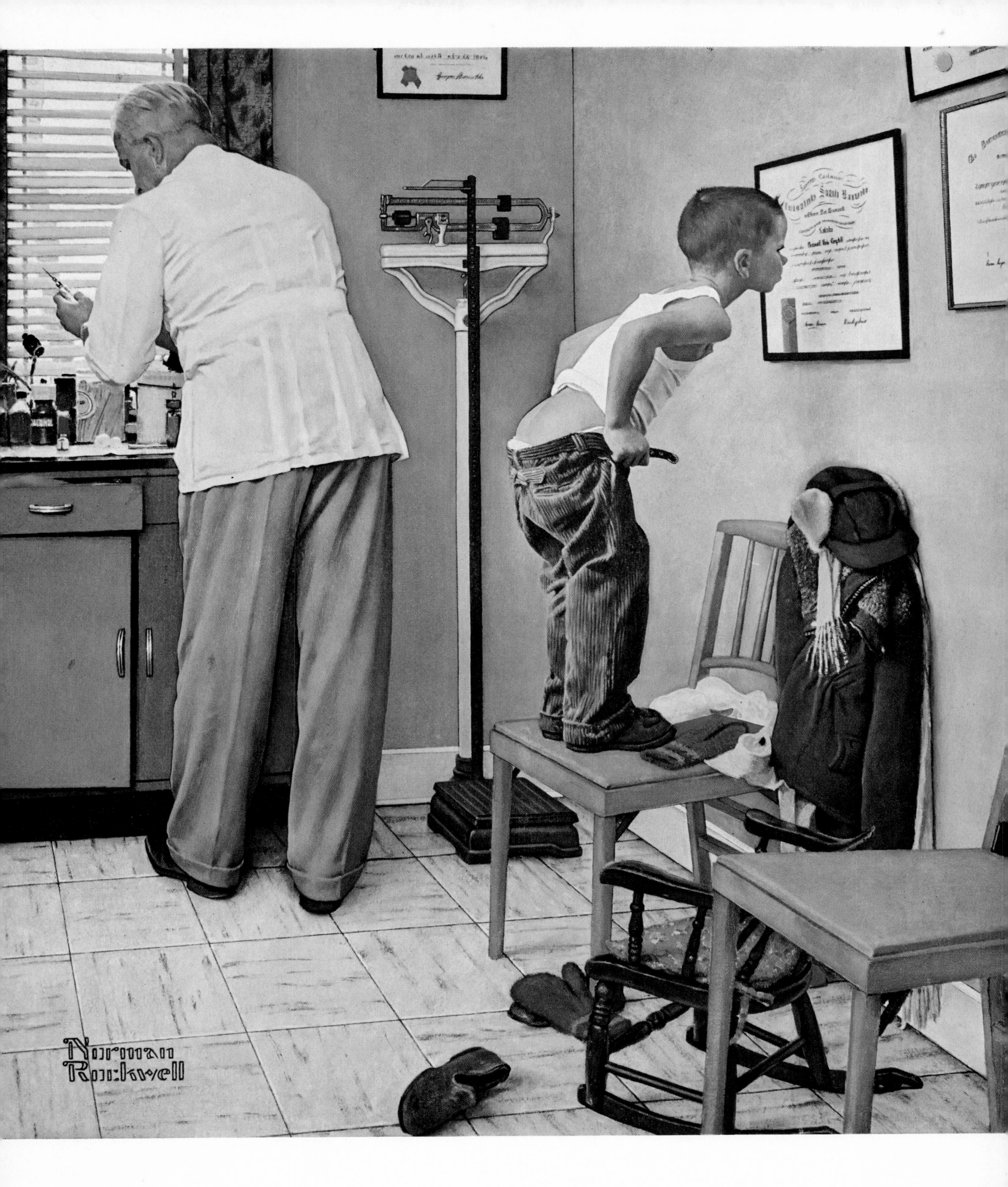
Norman
Rockwell

The first sketch. I had wanted to do a picture contrasting a diminutive jockey and an immense track official for a long time. The jockeys "weigh out" before a race, "weigh in" after a race.

This cover almost led me off the straight and narrow path. While photographing Eddie Arcaro, who posed for the jockey, at Santa Anita race track, I bet $2.00 on a horse and won $140. I thought perhaps I'd give up painting for betting. But I spent almost the entire $140 buying refreshments for the reporters in the press box, who had placed the bet for me.

The final sketch, made at Santa Anita. The changes between this and the first sketch were dictated by my observations of the actual scene.

Preliminary studies in black and white oil paint of Eddie Arcaro and Mr. James Mower, who posed for the track steward. I made them chiefly to work out the character of the steward.

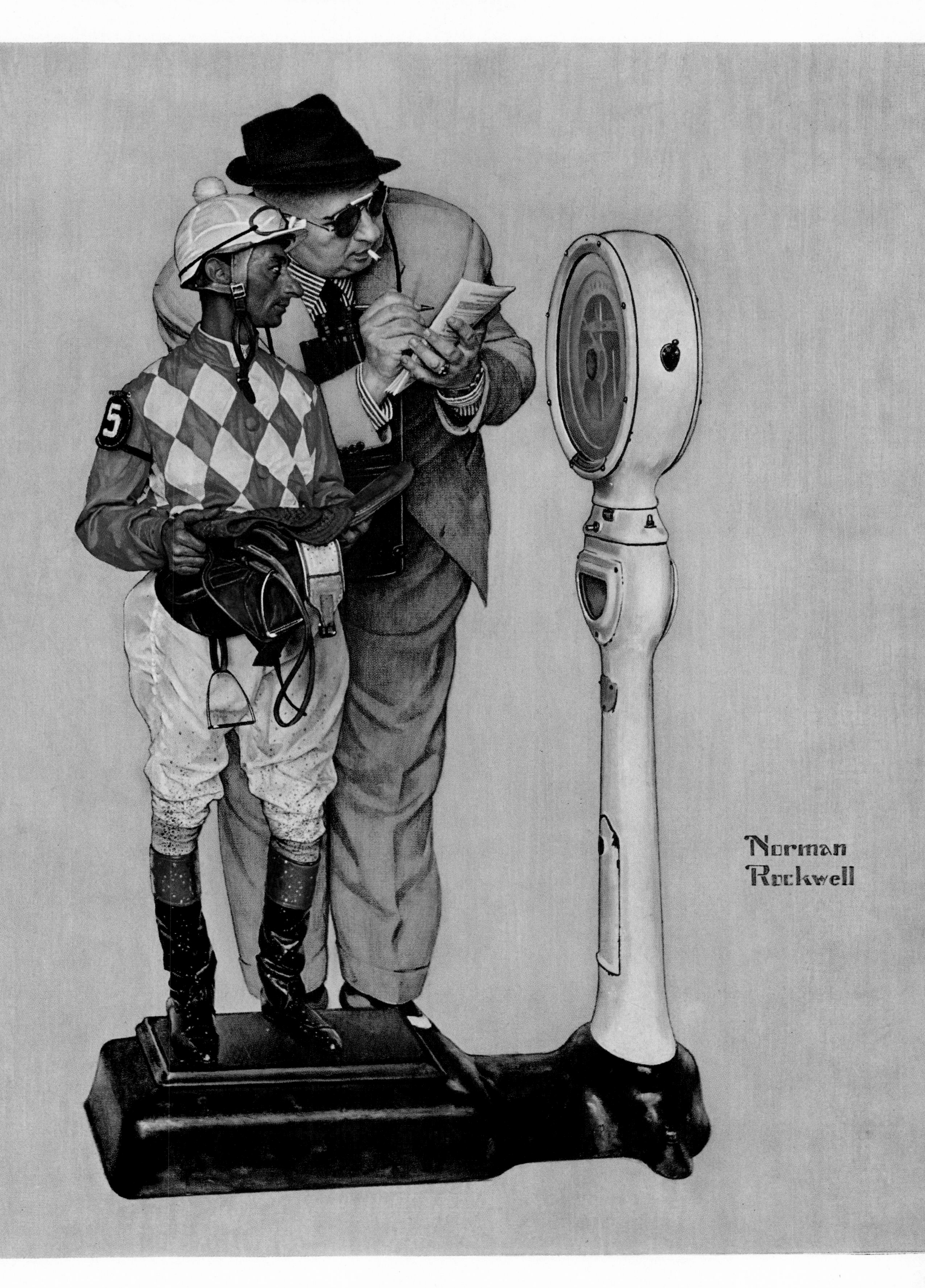
5
Norman
Rockwell

The first sketch. I ran away from home when I was a kid in Mamaroneck and mooned around the shore, kicking stones and watching the whitecaps on Long Island Sound. Pretty soon it began to get dark and a cold wind sprang up and moaned in the trees. So I went home.

Well, I painted this one twice too. It tires me just thinking about all the covers I've painted over. I changed the background from an urban Howard Johnson's to a rural lunchroom because I wanted to convey the idea that the kid had got well out of town before being apprehended. I found a new model for the counterman because I thought a jaded, worldly type would be more understanding than a young fellow.

SPECIAL TODAY
SpaGHetti +
MeaT balls -
Norman Rockwell

SCOVILL, PHOTOGRAPHER

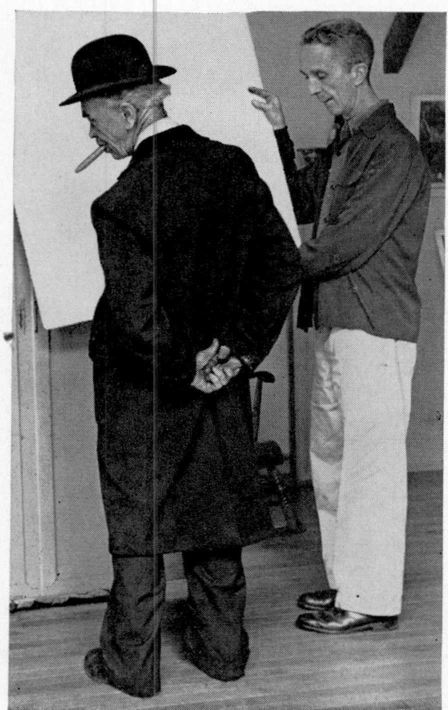

Tom Carey, the gentleman chatting with me in the photograph above and posing for me in the one to the left, is the person who really interests me in this cover. Here in Stockbridge he carried the mail in his horse and buggy from the railroad station to the post office for fifty years or more. During the summer he drives tourists about the countryside in his surrey, pointing out the places of interest—the old Mission House, the Indian graveyard—with his whip, and every so often stopping his horse so that the tourists can enjoy a particularly fine view of the blue-green, rolling Berkshires. Mr. Carey won't have a television set in his house because he says it would interfere with his reading: Shakespeare, history, politics. He is an authority on horses. A scholar and a gentleman.

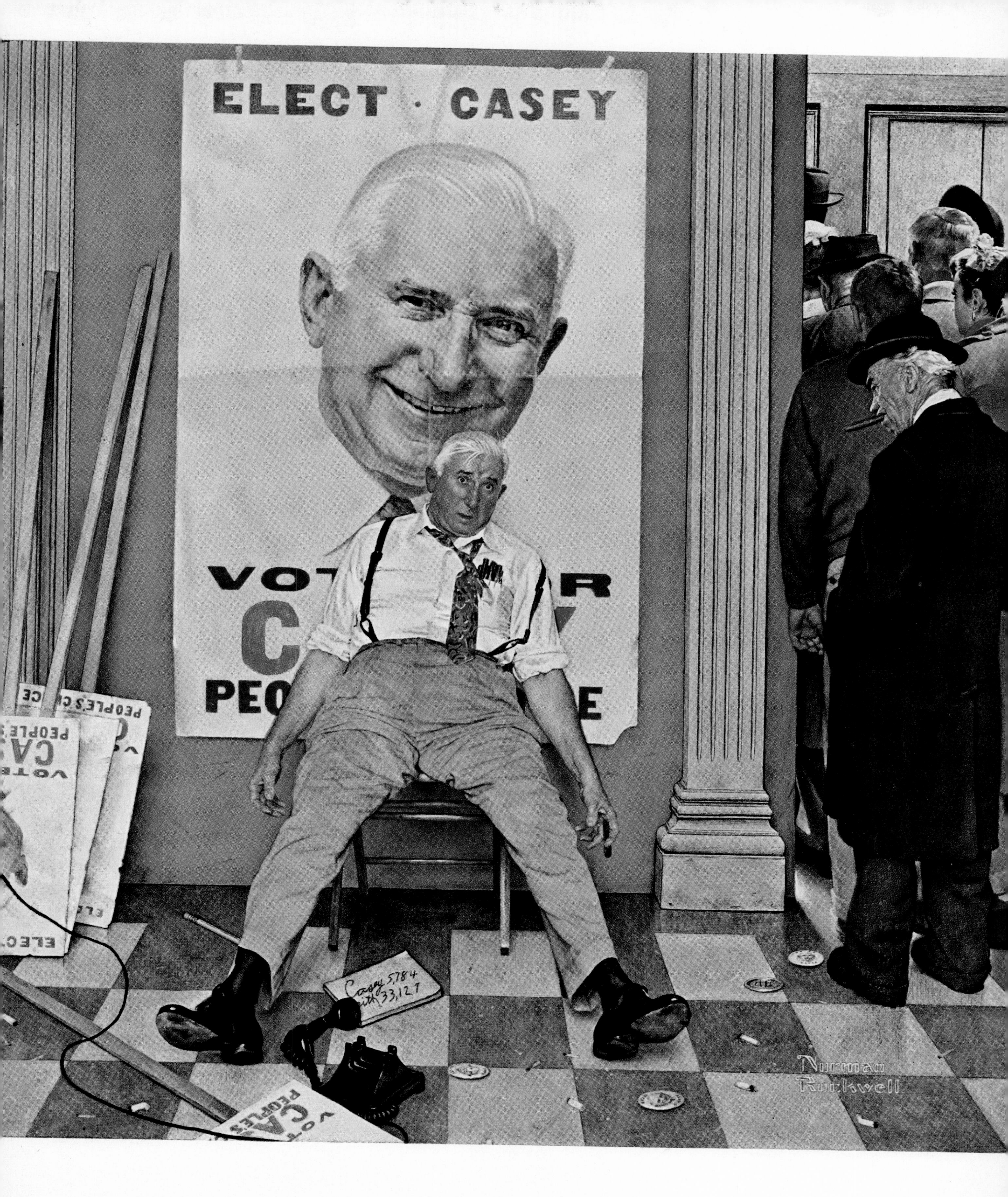
ELECT · CASEY
Casey 5,784
33,127
Norman Rockwell

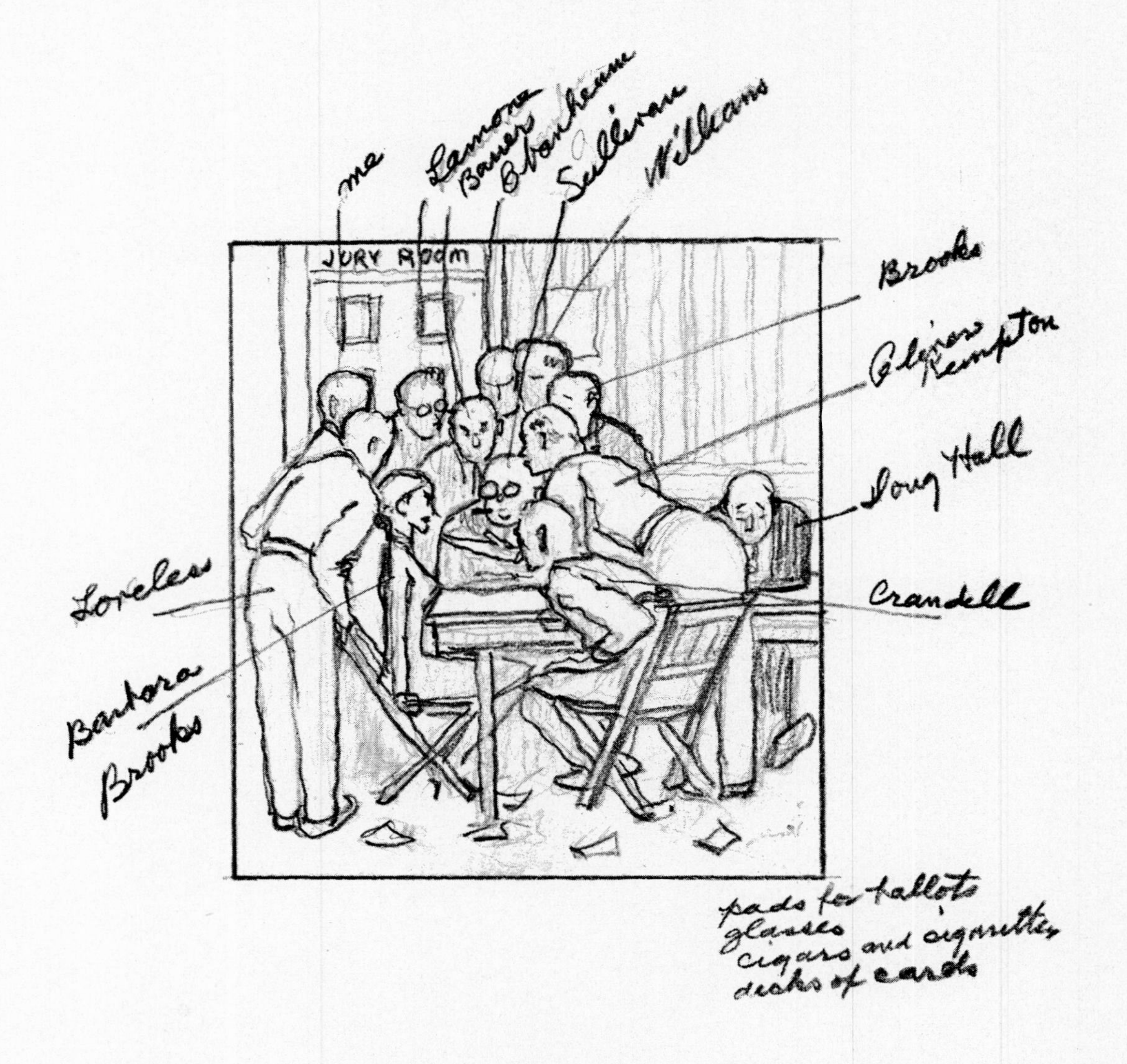

The first sketch. The names written around the margins are of people whom I thought I might use as models for the various characters in the painting. Selecting the right models is extremely important; I tell the story through the characters. One of the reasons I prefer to live in a small town rather than a city is that in a small town I know just about everybody and just about everybody knows me. So when I begin to select my models for a picture there are a large number of people whose faces I am acquainted with. And because they know me, most are willing to pose—all, in fact; no one has refused yet. The characters in this cover are a pretty good cross-section of the people of Stockbridge. There are a couple of ringers—the man with the mustache standing beside the sleeping juryman is Bob Brooks, an art director in a New York advertising agency; the lady in a man's world is his wife.

JURY ROOM
JURY
JURY ROOM
norman rockwell

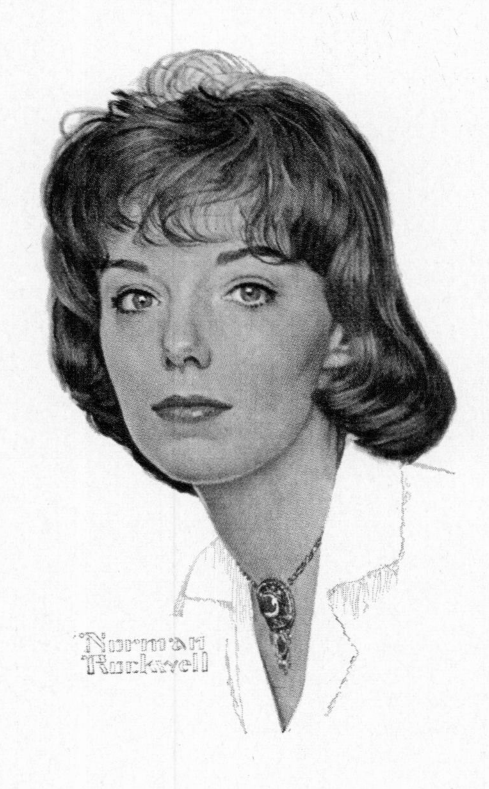

Nobody seemed to notice it, but the woman in this cover is too young to be the mother of those children. My daughter-in-law, Gail, was the model. She remarked on the incongruity, but consented to pose anyway. That's her again in the painting above, done to illustrate a recent story in the *Post*. I always used to say I couldn't paint pretty girls, but I don't know now. . . . In painting this cover I used a technique which I customarily do not use. I made a careful drawing and then brushed light washes of color over it. I can use this technique only when the people are silhouetted against the light. Then the light on their faces is diffused and casts few dark shadows. When the light comes from in front of the face, as in most of my covers, the variation of light and shade and thus of color is more pronounced, and a wash of color will not render it. . . . The scene outside the window is an exact reproduction of the view from my studio window.

Norman
Rockwell

Studies of some of the characters, made while painting the cover. I had the most trouble with the pirate at the bottom of the tree. As you can see, I tried a Puritan, a jolly buccaneer, and a rather respectable pirate. At the last, after weeks of struggle, I returned to the original pirate. Most of the difficulty sprang from my reluctance to begin the family with such a disreputable, fierce, coarse character.

The preliminary charcoal drawing. Although there are many differences between this and the finished painting, they do not reflect the difficulties I had with this picture. I painted the tree twice; the background, a number of times. My chief problem was finding the right characters to hang on the tree, however. In some instances, I tried three or four different characters before I hit upon the right one. Color was another problem. I had to balance the colors; I couldn't bunch all the bright colors in one spot, all the drab ones in another. The hats saved the situation.

a Family Tree by norman rockwell

Years ago in Westminster Abbey I happened to glance up at one of the great stained-glass windows and see an old craftsman high up on a scaffold, repairing the window. At the time I thought the scene would make a good *Post* cover. But until last year I never got around to attempting it. It did not turn out very well. No matter how hard I tried, I could not capture in paint the luminous radiance of a stained-glass window. I now think that what prevented me was that spot of dead white where the craftsman has removed the panes. It makes the rest of the window look opaque, blackens it, dims its luminous radiance. It is certainly possible to paint a stained-glass window but perhaps not with a spot of stark white in the center.

Norman
Rockwell

From these photographs I pieced together the figures of the girl and the sailor in the painting, selecting an arm from one photograph, a leg from another, the tilt of a head from one, a hand from another. Gen Melia, a movie starlet, posed for the girl. That's me in the lower left corner of the painting.

PHOTOGRAPHS BY ROBERT SCOTT STUDIO

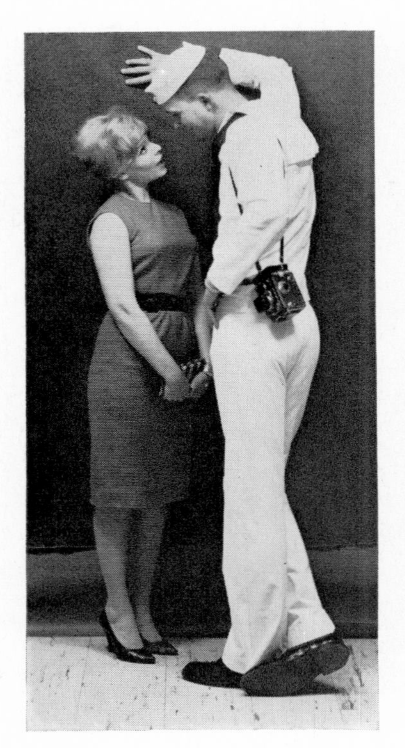

TH AV
W54 ST
norman rockwell

MY STUDIO TODAY

1. *Art books;* 2. *Print of Michelangelo's statue of Moses;* 3. *Print of Botticelli's "Primavera";* 4. *My sketch for a possible poster;* 5. *Original by American poster artist Edward Penfield;* 6. *Charcoal sketch by me;* 7. *Sketch of Gail;* 8. *Vermeer's "A Street in Delft";* 9. *Caravaggio print;* 10. *Print of Canaletto;* 11. *Pencil drawing of Louisa May Alcott;* 12. *Print of Rembrandt;* 13. *Color sketch by me for* Post *cover;* 14. *Prints of my "Golden Rule" cover;* 15. *Color print I picked up in Paris—do not know the artist;* 16. *Print of drawing by Holbein;* 17. *Picasso;* 18. *Rembrandt original etching called the "Hundred Guilder Print";* 19. *Bellini's "Saint Francis";* 20. *Rembrandt "Self-Portrait";* 21. *Original oil by Howard Pyle;* 22. *Brueghel's "The Parable of the Blind";* 23. *Dürer prints;* 24. *Indo-Chinese mask;* 25. *Color print of Bosch;* 26. *Detail of Caravaggio;* 27. *Abstract painting by Mary.*

My home and studio in Stockbridge.

These photographs of my studio were taken by my friend Bill Scovill, who has worked for me for many years.

My etching press.

A Spanish wood carving.

I PAINT THE GOLDEN RULE

Most of the time I try to entertain with my *Post* covers. But once in a while I get an uncontrollable urge to say something serious.

Like everyone else, I'm concerned with the world situation, and like everyone else, I'd like to contribute something to help. The only way I can contribute is through my pictures. So for a long time I had been trying to think of a subject that might be of some help.

Then one day (I don't know why or how) I suddenly got the idea that the Golden Rule — "Do unto Others as You Would Have Them Do unto You" — was the subject I was looking for. Right away I got intensely excited. But how could I picture the Golden Rule? I began to make all sorts of sketches. Then I remembered that down in the cellar of my studio was the ten-foot-long charcoal drawing of my United Nations picture, which I had never finished. I hauled it upstairs. In it I had tried to depict all the peoples of the world gathered together. That was just what I wanted to express about the Golden Rule.

I spent almost five months painting the picture. It was an enormous amount of work. But I never got discouraged about it and, right or wrong, I never stopped thinking that it was worthwhile.

The charcoal drawing of my United Nations picture: the Security Council in session, behind them the peoples of the world, for whom the deliberations of the Council mean peace or war, the chance to live their lives in happiness or in misery. I failed to carry this picture further, not because I had lost faith in the UN, but because I had lost confidence in my ability to express what I had wanted to say in the picture. When I decided to attempt a picture illustrating the Golden Rule and, remembering this charcoal, hauled it out of the cellar and looked at it, I immediately felt that in the grouping of the peoples of the world behind the delegates was the basis for my picture illustrating the Golden Rule.

The paste-up from the UN charcoal. I had a photograph taken of the charcoal; then I cut out some of the figures and arranged them on a piece of cardboard to see if the idea was viable. It was amazing how everything just seemed to fall into place. The two mothers holding their children seemed to express exactly what I was trying to say about the Golden Rule. Using them as the basis of my composition, I introduced new figures. Of the twenty-eight heads in the finished painting, eight were taken from the UN charcoal.

August 19, 1960. The first version of the preliminary drawing in Wolff pencil.

September 3. I wanted to include people of every race, creed, and color, depicting them with dignity and respect.

September 28. The final version of the drawing. Though I had not solved all the problems, I felt I should start the painting.

September 30. The first day's work on the painting. I was laying in the heads roughly.

October 1.

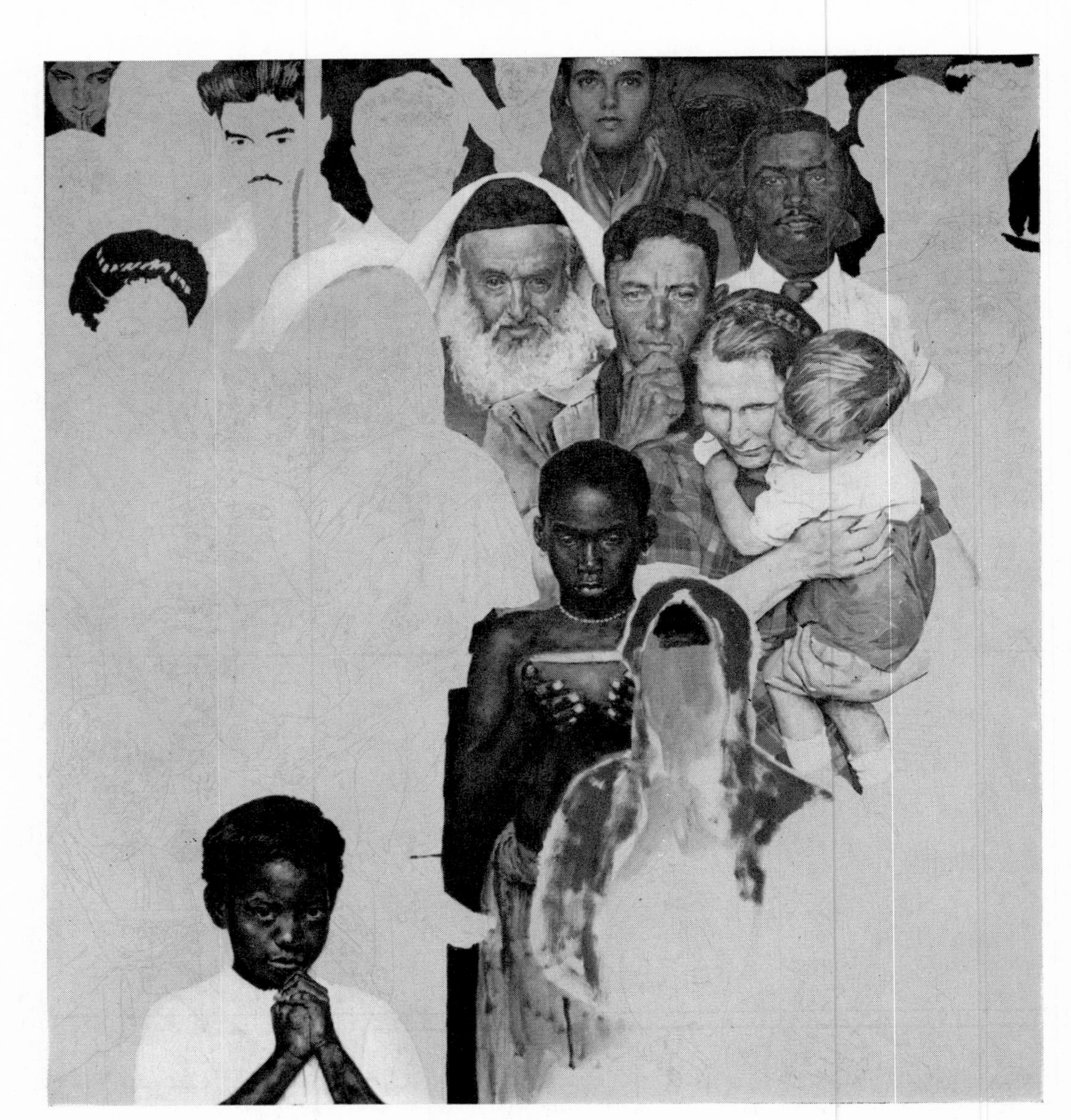

October 3. A painting always progresses rapidly while I am laying it in roughly.

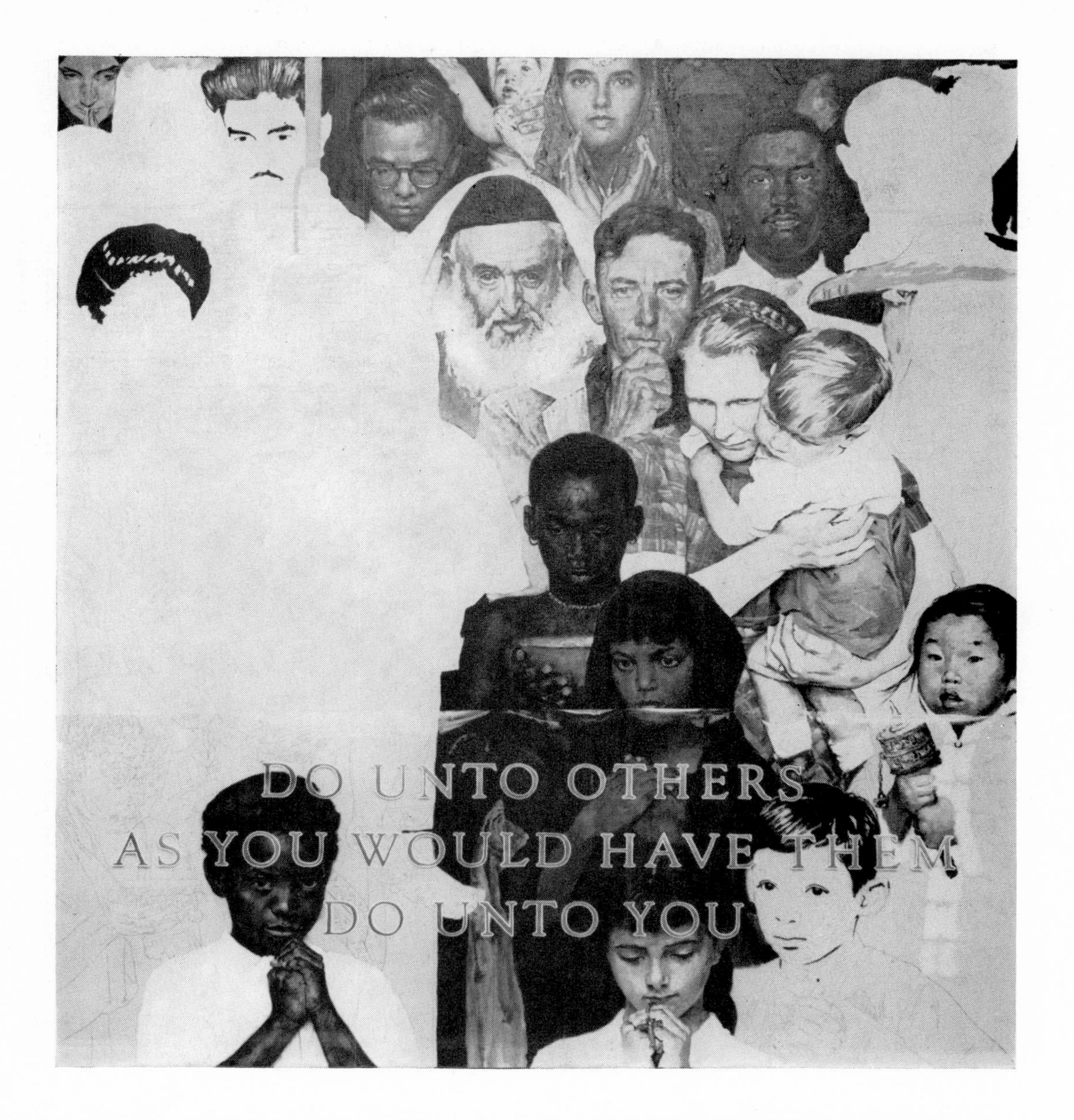

October 15. The Golden Rule is lettered on a cellophane overlay. I did not paint it on until the picture was finished.

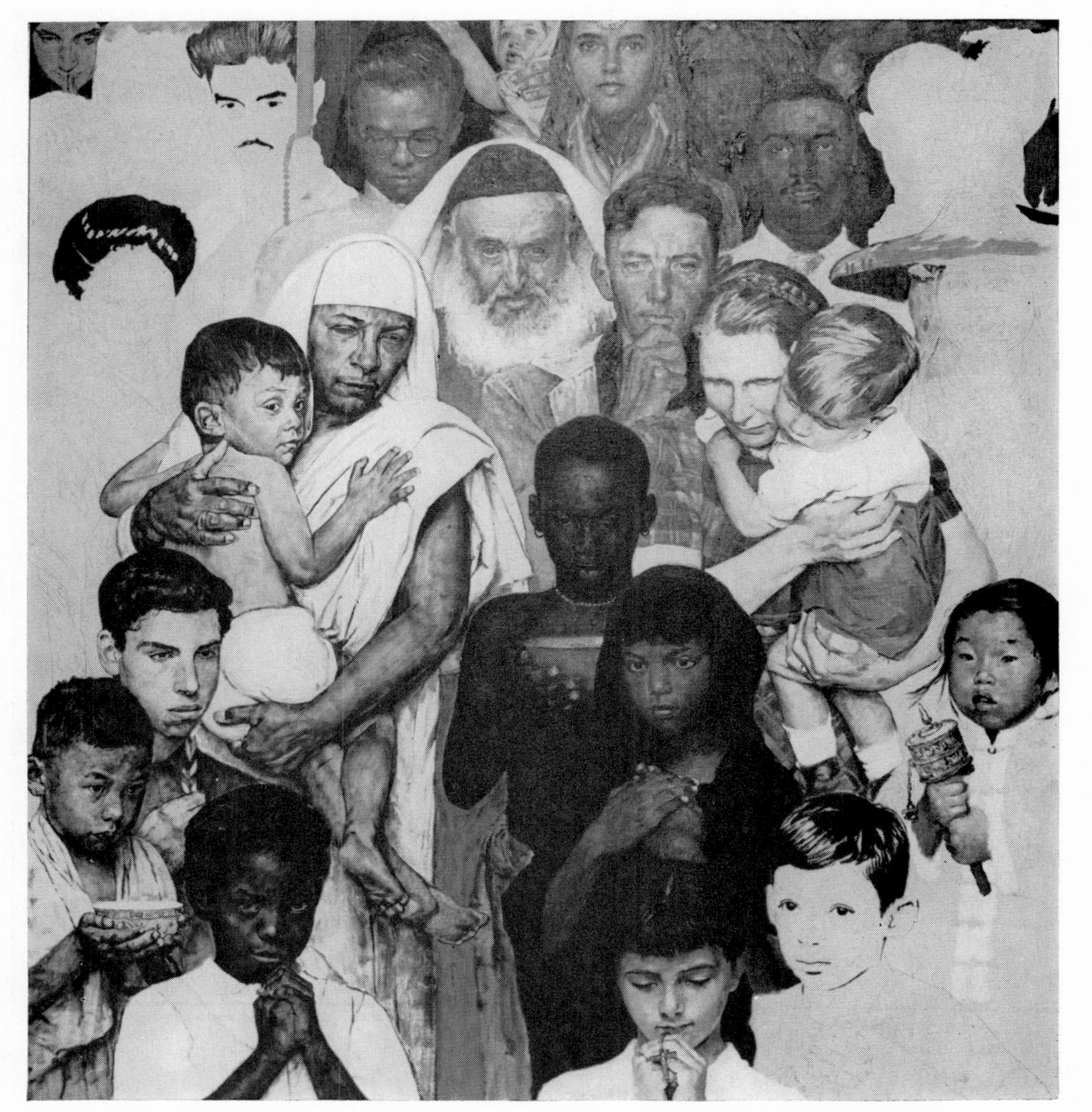

October 18.

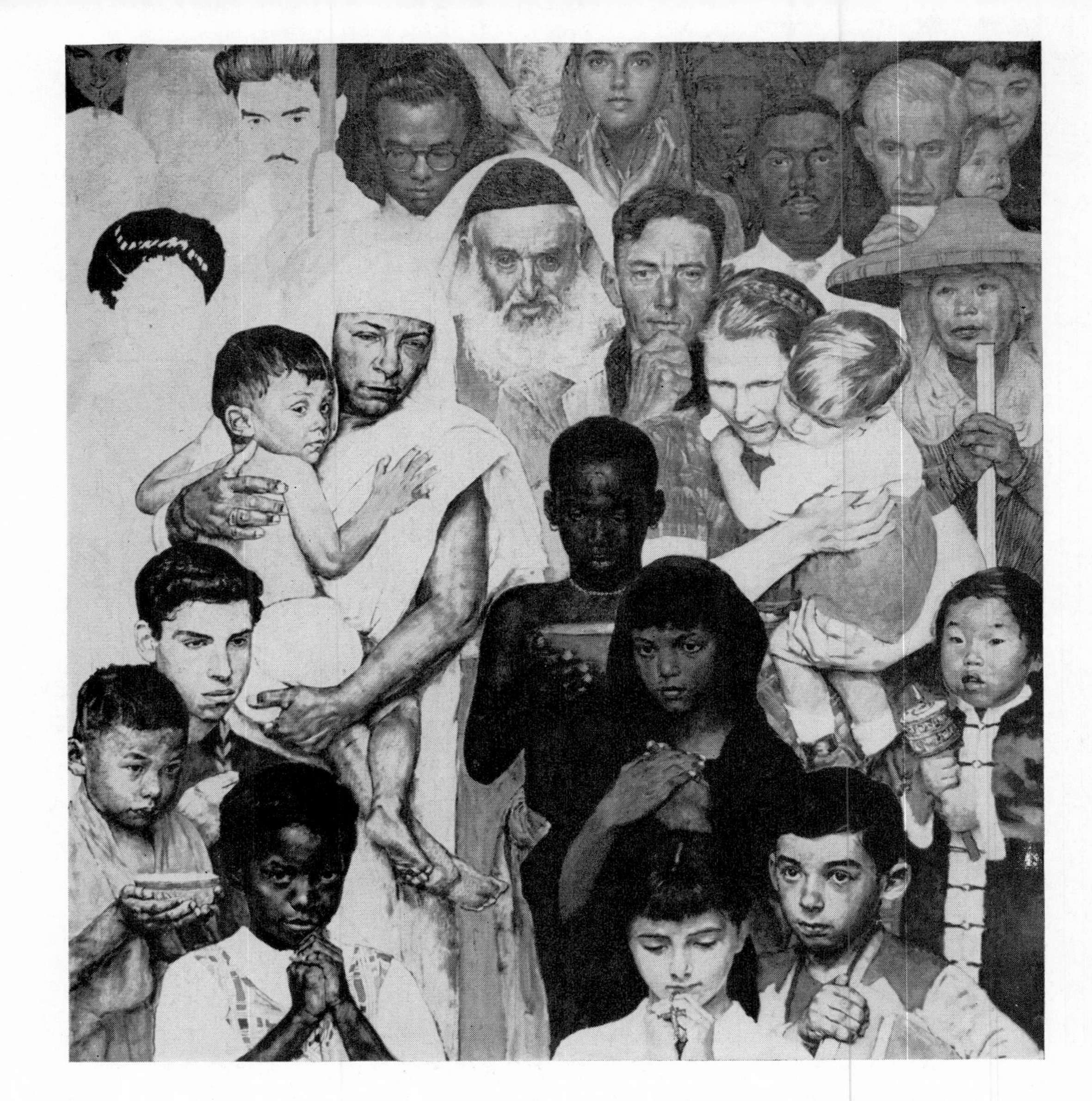

October 20.

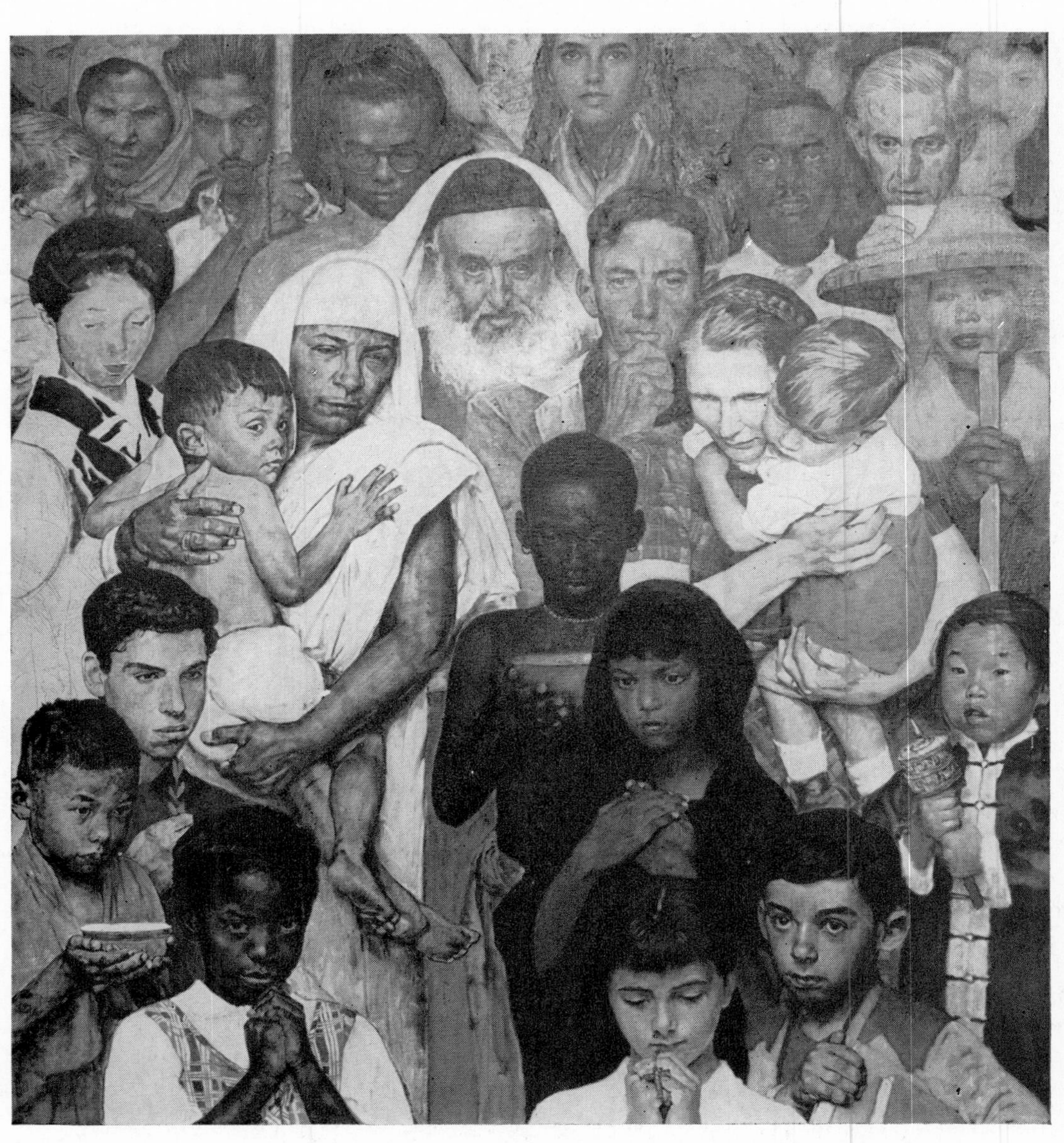

October 22. The painting progresses more slowly now. I am working out the subtle relationships of color and tone.

November 2. I am still making changes in an attempt to tell the story more clearly, with greater impact.

November 30. Each head must have a character of its own and yet contribute to the over-all conception. I finished the painting January 8, 1961.

THE GOLDEN RULE IS COMMON TO ALL RELIGIONS

BUDDHISM. Hurt not others with that which pains yourself. *Udanavarga.*

CHRISTIANITY. All things whatsoever ye would that men should do to you, do ye even so to them: for this is the law and the prophets. *Bible, St. Matthew.*

CONFUCIANISM. Is there any one maxim which ought to be acted upon throughout one's whole life? Surely the maxim of lovingkindness is such—Do not unto others what you would not they should do unto you. *Analects.*

HEBRAISM. What is hurtful to yourself do not to your fellow man. That is the whole of the Torah and the remainder is but commentary. Go learn it. *Talmud.*

HINDUISM. This is the sum of duty: do naught to others which if done to thee, would cause thee pain. *Mahabharata.*

ISLAM. No one of you is a believer until he loves for his brother what he loves for himself. *Traditions.*

JAINISM. In happiness and suffering, in joy and grief, we should regard all creatures as we regard our own self, and should therefore refrain from inflicting upon others such injury as would appear undesirable to us if inflicted upon ourselves. *Yogashastra.*

SIKHISM. As thou deemest thyself so deem others. Then shalt thou become a partner in heaven. *Kabir.*

TAOISM. Regard your neighbor's gain as your own gain: and regard your neighbor's loss as your own loss. *T'ai Shang Kan Ying P'ien.*

ZOROASTRIANISM. That nature only is good when it shall not do unto another whatever is not good for its own self. *Dadistan-i-dinik.*

"We have committed the Golden Rule to memory,
let us now commit it to life."
EDWIN MARKHAM

DO UNTO OTHERS
AS YOU WOULD HAVE THEM
DO UNTO YOU
Norman Rockwell